ENGLISH MEN OF LETTERS

WALTER PATER

ENGLISH MEN OF LETTERS

WALTER PATER

BY

A. C. BENSON

FELLOW OF MAGDALENE COLLEGE, CAMBRIDGE

LONDON: MACMILLAN & CO., LIMITED
NINETEEN HUNDRED AND SIX

PREFACE

In the absence of any official biography of Walter Pater, it has been necessary to collect information as to the events of his life from his relatives and friends. My thanks are due, in the first place, to Miss Pater and Miss Clara Pater, his sisters, who have given me the most kind and courteous assistance throughout; to Dr. Shadwell, Provost of Oriel, Pater's oldest friend and literary executor, of whose sympathy and interest it is impossible to speak too gratefully; to Dr. Bussell, Vice-Principal of Brasenose, who has communicated to me many important particulars; to Mr. Herbert Warren, President of Magdalen; to Dr. Daniel, Provost of Worcester, and Mrs. Daniel; to Mr. Basil Champneys; to Mr. Humphry Ward, formerly Fellow of Brasenose; to Mr. Douglas Ainslie; to Miss Paget (Vernon Lee), and others who have put their recollections at my disposal; to Mr. Edmund Gosse, who has permitted me to use his published materials; to Mr. Howard Sturgis and Mr. C. Fairfax Murray for careful criticism; to Miss Beatrice Layman, who has given me invaluable help in verification and correction.

The books and articles which I have consulted, and to some of which reference is made in the following pages, are the original editions of Pater's volumes, of various dates, and the Collected Edition of his works, edited by Dr. Shadwell, 1902-1904 (Macmillan and Co.); *Essays from the Guardian*, privately printed in 1896, and since published, 1901 (Macmillan and Co.); *A Short History of Modern English Literature*, 1898 (Heinemann); *Critical Kit-Kats*, 1896 (Heinemann), and an article in the *Dictionary of National Biography*, 1895 (Smith, Elder, and Co.), by Mr. Edmund Gosse; *Walter Pater*, by Mr. Ferris Greenslet, in the *Contemporary Men of Letters Series*, 1904 (Heinemann); an essay, *Walter Pater*, in *Studies in Prose and Verse*, by Mr. Arthur Symons, 1904 (J. M. Dent); and an article in the *Fortnightly Review*, "The Work of Mr. Pater," by Lionel Johnson, September 1894 (Chapman and Hall).

A. C. B.

CONTENTS

WALTER PATER

CHAPTER I

EARLY LIFE

VERY little is recorded and still less is known about
the pedigree of Pater. It is only in the main line of
families that are established in ancestral estates, and
whose home is inherited by a succession of heirs, that
family traditions are apt to accumulate.

The name Pater is uncommon in England, and not at
all uncommon in Holland, the Dutch frequently latin-
ising their names; this, and the fact that a Dutch
Admiral of that name settled in England at the time
of William of Orange, made some members of the Pater
family think they were originally of Dutch extraction;
but this has never been verified. In a journey through
Holland, Walter Pater was much interested in a
picture at Amsterdam, by Van der Helst, of archers,
with a tablet giving the names of the winners in a
contest of skill; at the top of the list stands the
name Pater.

The forefathers of Walter Pater were living at Weston-
Underwood, near Olney in Buckinghamshire, the home
of Cowper, in the eighteenth century, and some verses
in the handwriting of the poet were preserved by their
descendants. One of the Olney Paters emigrated to
America; and here Richard Glode Pater, the father

of Walter Pater, was born. Early in the nineteenth
century the household returned to England, settling
at Shadwell, between Wapping and Stepney; and
here Richard Pater practised medicine, careless of
money and success alike, a man of unobtrusive benevolence, labouring at the relief of suffering among
poor people, who often could not afford to pay for
his advice. Here he married a Miss Hill: four
children were born to him, two sons, of whom the
elder, William Thompson Pater, became a doctor and
died in 1887, and two daughters. Walter Horatio
Pater was born in 1839, on August 4th. Dr. Richard
Pater died so early that his famous son could hardly
remember him. After his death the household moved
to Enfield, and here at an old house, now demolished,
with a big garden, in the neighbourhood of Chase
Side, the children were brought up. This quiet life
was varied by visits to a place called Fish Hall, near
Hadlow in Kent, the residence of Walter Pater's
cousin and godmother, Mrs. Walter May.

It is stated in biographical notices of Pater that for
some generations the sons of the family had been
brought up as Catholics, the daughters as Anglicans.
But this has been too much insisted upon; as a matter
of fact the Roman Catholicism in the family was of
late date. Walter Pater's great-grandfather was a
convert, having married a lady of great piety and sweetness, whose mother's maiden name was Gage, belonging to an old Roman Catholic family in Suffolk.
Richard Pater, Walter's father, quitted the Roman
Church before his marriage, and adopted no particular form of faith; and Walter Pater was brought up
as an Anglican.

At the age of fourteen the boy was sent to the
King's School, Canterbury, where he seems to have

been regarded at first as idle and backward; but he was popular in spite of an entire indifference to games. Not till he entered the sixth form did his intellectual ambition awaken.

It would be interesting to know something of the thoughts of this grave, silent, and friendly boy through the impressionable years; but, like many boys of ability, he was affected by a sensitive shyness, a reticence about his inner thoughts. Cheerful, lively, chattering children, who too often, alas! degenerate into the bores of later life, can generally talk easily and unaffectedly about their tastes and interests, and blithely reveal the slender sparkling stream of their thoughts. But with boys of perceptive and meditative temperaments it is mostly far otherwise. They find themselves overmastered by feelings which they cannot express, and which they are ashamed of trying to express for fear of being thought eccentric. Pater was always apt to be reticent about his own interior feelings, and confided them only to the more impersonal medium of his writings. He had no taste at any time for indulging in reminiscence, and tended rather to be the recipient of other people's thoughts, which he welcomed and interpreted with ready sympathy, than to be garrulous about the details of his own life, which, with characteristic humility, he was disposed to consider destitute of interest.

But one trait of character does undoubtedly emerge. He was instinctively inclined to a taste for symbolical ceremony of every kind. In the family circle he was fond of organising little processional pomps, in which the children were to move with decorous solemnity. He looked forward to taking orders in the Church of England; and this bias was strengthened by a visit he paid, as a little boy, to a house of some friends at

Hursley.   There he met Keble, who had a great
devotion to children.   Keble took a fancy to the quiet
serious child, walked with him, and spoke with him
of the religious life, in a way that made a deep impression on the boy's mind, though they never met again.

There are two of Pater's studies, *The Child in the
House* and *Emerald Uthwart*, with which it is obvious
that a certain autobiographical thread is interwoven.
But it is necessary to resist the temptation to take
either of them as in any sense a literal representation
of facts.   Rather it may be said that Pater's early
years supplied him with a delicate background of
reminiscence, upon which he embroidered a richer
ornament of dreamful thought, using, in his own
phrase, the finer sort of memory.

It is clear, however, that he was instinctively alive to
impressions of sense, and that his mind was early at
work observing and apprehending a certain quality in
things perceived and heard, which he was afterwards to
recognise as beauty.   He had few outbursts of high
spirits or unreasoning glee; it was rather a tranquil
current of somewhat critical enjoyment; but he was
sensitive to a whole troop of perceptions, of which the
normal child would hardly be conscious—the coolness of dark rooms on hot summer days, the carelessly
ordered garden, the branching trees, the small flowers,
so bright of hue, so formal of shape, the subtle
scents of the old house, the pot-pourri of the drawing-
room, the aroma of old leather in the library; for it
was about the house, the familiar rooms, that Pater's
memory persistently dwelt, rather than on the wider
prospect of field and hill.

There is a beautiful and interesting passage in which
Pater embalmed his view of the permanence of these
early impressions :—

"The perfume of the little flowers of the lime-tree fell
through the air upon them like rain; while time seemed to
move ever more slowly to the murmur of the bees in it, till it
almost stood still on June afternoons. How insignificant, at
the moment, seem the influences of the sensible things which
are tossed and fall and lie about us, so, or so, in the environment of early childhood. How indelibly, as we afterwards
discover, they affect us; with what capricious attractions and
associations they figure themselves on the white paper, the
smooth wax, of our ingenuous souls, as 'with lead in the rock
for ever,' giving form and feature, and as it were assigned house-
room in our memory, to early experiences of feeling and
thought, which abide with us ever afterwards, thus, and not
otherwise."

But he points out clearly enough that very little
that is critical is intermingled with the perceptions of
childhood :—

"It is false to suppose that a child's sense of beauty is de-
pendent on any choiceness or special fineness, in the objects
which present themselves to it, though this indeed comes to
be the rule with most of us in later life."

There were two strains of sentiment which he discerned to have chiefly coloured his childish thoughts.
One was "the visible, tangible, audible loveliness of
things . . . marking early the activity in him of a
more than customary sensuousness . . . which might
lead him, one day, how far!"

And then, too, the sorrow and suffering of the world
came home in dim glimpses to the child, as a thing
which was inextricably intertwined with the life of men
and animals alike. There was as yet no attempt to
harmonise the two dominant strains of feeling; they
were the two great facts for him—beauty and sorrow;
they seemed so distinct from, so averse to each other,
sorrow laying her pale hand so firmly on life, withering

it at its very source, and striking from it what was lovely and delectable. And yet he noted the pathetic attempt of beauty to reassert itself, as in the violets which grew on the child's grave, and drew their sweetness from sad mortality. And there came too the terror of death, the sad incidents of which imprint themselves with so sinister a horror on the tender mind. "At any time or place, in a moment, the faint atmosphere of the chamber of death would be breathed around him, and the image with the bound chin, the quaint smile, the straight, stiff feet, shed itself across the air upon the bright carpet, amid the gayest company, or happiest communing with himself."

These were the dreams of childhood, the unchecked visions of the sheltered and secluded home; at Canterbury came a wider, nobler, richer prospect of beauty. He found himself in that exquisite, irregular city, with its narrow streets; the mouldering gateways leading to the Close, where the huge Cathedral rises among a paradise of lawns and gardens; with the ancient clustering houses, of which some contain the gables and windows of the old monastic buildings, while some are mere centos of ancient stone, the ruins having been used for a quarry; some of mellow brick, with a comfortable Erastian air about them, speaking of the settled prosperity of eighteenth-century churchmanship; the whole tenderly harmonised by sun and rain into a picture of equable, dignified, English life, so that wherever the eye turned, it fell upon some delicate vignette full of grace and colour.

It is of this period that *Emerald Uthwart*, that strange fanciful story, holds certain reminiscences, but reminiscences coloured and tranquillised by the backward-looking eye. "If at home there had been nothing great, here, to boyish sense, one seems diminished to nothing at all, amid the grand waves, wave upon wave, of patiently-wrought stone ; the daring height, the daring severity, of the innumerable, long, upward, ruled lines, rigidly bent just at last, in due place, into the reserved grace of the perfect Gothic arch ; the peculiar daylight which seemed to come from further than the light outside."

But still it must be borne in mind that all this was rather perceived, noted, and accumulated in the boyish mind than expressed or even consciously felt. The scenes, the surroundings of boyhood just inscribe themselves upon the mind, which seldom pauses to reflect or to criticise ; it is long after, in maturity, with the wistful and tender sense of the past, that the recollection, tranquilly recalled, is tinged with poetry and sweetness. There was little consciousness in Pater's boyish days of how deep these things were settling into his mind, and still less foreshadowing of the magic power that would enable him to recall and express them in melodious words. The only definite artistic influence under which he is known to have fallen in his school-days is the influence of Ruskin, whom he read as a boy of nineteen. It is possible to trace this influence in Pater's mature style ; there is something of the same glowing use of words, something of the same charming *naïveté* and transparency in the best passages of both ; but whereas Ruskin is remarkable for prodigality, Pater is remarkable for restraint ; Ruskin drew his vocabulary from a hundred sources, and sent it pouring down in a bright cascade, whereas Pater chose more and more to refine his use of words, to indicate rather than to describe. Ruskin's, in fact, is a natural style and Pater's is an artificial one ; but he undoubtedly received a strong impulse from Ruskin in the direction of ornamental expression ; and a still stronger impulse in the direc-

tion of turning a creative force into the criticism of
beautiful things—a vein of subjective criticism, in
fact.

In June 1858 Pater entered Queen's College, Oxford.
He was a commoner, but held an exhibition awarded
him from Canterbury.

Queen's College was founded in 1340 by Robert
Eglesfield, a chaplain to Queen Philippa, who largely
supplemented her priest's endowment. The medieval buildings have entirely disappeared, and the
college consists of a great Italian court, designed by
Hawksmoor, Wren's pupil, with a fine pillared screen
dividing it from the High Street, and a smaller court
behind. The Chapel is a stately classical building,
designed by Wren himself, and considered by him one
of his most successful works. It is rich with seven-
teenth-century glass by Van Linge, and dignified woodwork. The Library is a magnificent room, with much
carving by Grinling Gibbons, certain panels of which
are almost perfect examples of freedom of form with
an underlying serenity of design. The lofty Hall might
have come straight out of an Italian picture, and the
mysterious gallery at the west end, opening by cur-
tained porches on balconies of delicate ironwork, seems
designed to be crowded by fantastic smiling persons in
rich garments.

It was a definitely ecclesiastical foundation, and preserved a larger number of quaint names and symbolical
customs than are preserved at other colleges; such as
announcing dinner by the sound of the trumpet, and
the retention of the name Taberdar for scholars. Pater
lived a very secluded and unobtrusive life in the back
quadrangle, associating with a few friends; he worked
at classics with moderate diligence, amusing himself with
metaphysics, which even in his school-days had begun

to exercise an attraction over him. There is nothing
which would lead one to suppose that his thoughts
turned in the direction of either art or literature. It
has been stated in some notices of his life that Jowett
discovered Pater's abilities, and gave him gratuitous
teaching. From this it would seem to be inferred
that Pater found a pecuniary difficulty in providing
himself with adequate instruction, which was not the
case. The explanation is simply that Jowett, as Professor of Greek, offered to look over the Greek compositions and essays of any members of his class who
cared to submit them to him, and Pater took advan-
tage, like many other men, of the offer. Jowett
indeed divined a peculiar quality in Pater's mind,
saying to him one day, in one of those lean simple
phrases that seem to have exercised so remarkably
stimulating a power over his pupils' minds, "I think
you have a mind that will come to great eminence."
But Pater failed to do himself justice in his examina-
tions, taking only a second-class in the Final Classical
Schools in 1862. For a couple of years he lived in
lodgings in High Street, and took pupils. In 1864
he was elected to a Fellowship at Brasenose, where
he immediately went into residence.

Pater's mother had died while he was at school
at Canterbury. His aunt, an unmarried sister of his
father, came to take charge of the family in her
place. When Pater went up to Oxford, his aunt
took his sisters to Heidelberg and Dresden, to complete their education, and it was there that Pater
spent his long vacations. But he made no German
acquaintances, and lived a life of quiet work and
interior speculation; he did not even acquire a conversational knowledge of German. In 1869 he took
a tour in Italy with Mr. Charles Lancelot Shadwell,

his closest and most intimate friend. They visited
Ravenna, Pisa, and Florence, and it was then that
art became for him the chief preoccupation of his
inner life.

Up till this time there is little hint of the line on
which he was afterwards to develop. Such attempts as
he had made in the direction of literary expression were
mostly destroyed by himself at a later date ; the only
thing which survives is a curious little study called
Diaphaneitè, which is dated July 1864, and is now included in the *Miscellaneous Studies*. This was written as
a paper to be read aloud to a small society called the
"Old Mortality," of which he was a member, and
to which many remarkable men belonged. The germ
of his later writings can here be clearly discerned, but
there is a certain dry compression about the little
essay which is very unlike the later ornate manner.
It is crammed almost too full of thought, and the evolution has a certain uneasiness arising from the omission
of easy transitions. In the essay Pater endeavours to
indicate a certain type of character presenting neither
breadth nor colour, but a narrow and potent sincerity.

"That fine edge of light, where the elements of our moral
nature refine themselves to the burning point." "It seeks to
value everything at its eternal worth, not adding to it, or
taking from it, the amount of influence it may have for or
against its own special scheme of life."

"Its ethical result is an intellectual guilelessness, or in-
tegrity, that instinctively prefers what is direct and clear, lest
one's own confusion and intransparency should hinder the
transmission from without of light that is not yet inward." [1]

---

[1] One circumstance, which gives the piece a special and
personal interest, deserves to be mentioned. It is not dis-
puted that the temperament there indicated was carefully
delineated from Pater's intimate friend, C. L. Shadwell, now
Provost of Oriel.

In such strict compressed sentences Pater traces his ideal of intellectual and moral sincerity ; but the value of the paper is that, in the first place, it shows a power of acute and subtle psychological analysis, and in the second place it expresses with difficult wistfulness the ideal with which the young student meant to approach the world. To that ideal he was unfailingly true. He meant to know, to weigh, to consider ; not to see things through the eyes of others, but to follow step by step the golden clue that ran for him through the darkness. It indicates a fearlessness, an independence of mind, which few achieve so early, and which fewer still have the patience to follow out.

In these years Pater's chief interest, apart from his prescribed work, was in philosophy, which naturally led him to the study of German authors ; and here he fell under the influence of Goethe. Goethe came to be for Pater the " true illustration of the speculative temper," " one to whom every moment of life brought its contribution of experimental, individual knowledge ; by whom no touch of the world of form, colour, and passion was disregarded."

It is necessary to bear in mind that there were two distinct strains in Pater's mind : there was on the one hand a strong impulse towards transcendental philosophy, a desire to discern as far as possible the absolute principles of life and being. He hankered after a certain clearness of view, a theory which could explain for him the strange confusion of the intellectual life, where so many currents of the human spirit seem not so much to blend, as to check and oppose each other. The human mind seems to be haunted by a conception of ultimate truth, and to deal in intuitions which appear to hint at a possible solution ; but the higher in the scale of perception that a mind is, the more complex are the influences which seem to distract it.

On the other hand there was a strong attraction to precise and definite types of beauty. Pater was checked in his metaphysical researches by his acute sense of the relativity of thought, by his apprehension of the sacredness of beauty, by his deep sensitiveness to art. What he longed for was a reasonable formula, which could connect the two, which could make him feel that the same law was at work both in the region of beauty and in the region of philosophical truth. "It is no vague scholastic abstraction," he wrote, "that will satisfy the speculative instinct in our modern minds. Who would change the colour or curve of a rose-leaf for that . . . colourless, formless, intangible being Plato put so high?"

The influence of his metaphysical studies is seen in his first published writing, a fragment on Coleridge, considered as a philosopher, which appeared in the *Westminster Review* in 1866. This was afterwards reprinted in the *Appreciations* in 1889, with a passage added on the poetry of Coleridge, which he had contributed, in 1883, as a biographical introduction to the selections from the poet in Ward's *English Poets*.

The first part of this essay traces the retrograde character of the philosophy of Coleridge, his rebellion against the patient generalisation of the scientific method. There are flashes of acute criticism, as when he points out that the chief faults of Coleridge's philosophical writings are in the first place their roughness, their lack of form; and in the second place the writer's excess of seriousness, "a seriousness arising not from any moral principle, but from a misconception of the perfect manner."

No doubt the reason why Coleridge as a philosopher

won such an influence in England was that he joined
to a deep grasp of transcendental metaphysics a somewhat tame acceptance of the orthodox religious position.   Here emerges the essential weakness of his
philosophy.   He accepted as reasonable assumptions
the orthodox views of revealed religion.   He made no
attempt to treat in a critical spirit the sources through
which this revelation was made; the result was that
the religious writers of the day—and it must be borne
in mind that the main current of intellectual interest
was in Coleridge's time religious rather than philosophical — welcomed Coleridge as a man who had
sounded the depths of metaphysical and speculative
inquiry, and had returned from his quest not a sceptic
nor a rationalist, but a convinced Christian.   After
such a triumph for religious feeling, his lesser hetero-
doxies were eagerly forgiven.

Pater does not dwell upon this side of Coleridge's influence; but there is no doubt that it deeply affected
his own religious thought.   He is believed at this time
to have cherished the scheme of becoming a Unitarian
minister; his metaphysical studies did not in fact
destroy his strong religious instinct, but only drew
him away for a time from the spell of association
and tradition which the Church exercised over him,
and to the domain of which he was eventually to
return.

The essay on Coleridge is mainly interesting, not
for its substance, subtle as it is, but for the fact that
it reveals the beginnings of Pater's style.   It is clear
that he is struggling hard with the German influence;
the terminology is technical, and a vague and dreamy
emotion seems to be moving somewhat stiffly in the
grip of metaphysical ideas; the sentences are long
and involved, and there is a great lack of lucidity of

construction, combined with a precision of expression, that produces a blurred and bewildering effect upon the mind.

It is impossible to believe that one who, like Pater, felt so strongly the sensuous influence of external beauty in art and nature, can have lingered long among abstractions. He never lost his interest in philosophy, but it became for him not so much a region into which he escaped from the actual world, as a region in which he could bring into line the vague suggestions of beauty and the laws of pure thought. He felt that beauty, while it haunted him, also distracted him; and while he could not resist its appeal to his emotional nature, he longed to be able to stand above it as well, and to see how it harmonised with more abstract conceptions; to arrive, indeed, at a certain serenity and tranquillity of thought, in which the perception of beauty might set, as it were, a sweet and solemn descant to the reasonable and sustained melody of the intellectual ideal.

Contact with practical life, together with his first sight of Italian art, turned Pater's thoughts gradually away from metaphysical speculation; and the final conversion came in his discovery of Otto Jahn's *Life of Winckelmann*, which opened to him a new prospect. The teaching of Goethe had begun to seem too passionate, too sensual; the idealism of Ruskin degenerated too much into sentiment, and forfeited balance and restraint; Hegel and Schelling were too remote from life, with all its colour, all its echoes; but in Winckelmann he found one who could devote himself to the passionate contemplation of beauty, without any taint or grossness of sense; who was penetrated by fiery emotion, but without any dalliance with feminine sentiment; whose sensitiveness

was preternaturally acute, while his conception was
cool and firm. Here, then, he discovered, or appeared
to himself to discover, a region in which beauty and
philosophy might unite in a high impassioned mood of
sustained intellectual emotion.

Brasenose College, with which Pater's life was to be
identified, is one of the sternest and severest in aspect
of Oxford colleges. It has no grove or pleasaunce to
frame its sombre antiquity in a setting of colour and
tender freshness. Its black and blistered front looks
out on a little piazza occupied by the stately mouldering dome of the Radcliffe Library ; beyond is the solid
front of Hertford, and the quaint pseudo-Gothic court
of All Souls. To the north lies a dark lane, over the
venerable wall of which looms the huge chestnut of
Exeter, full in spring of stiff white spires of heavy-
scented bloom. To the south a dignified modern
wing, built long after Pater's election, overlooks the
bustling High Street. To the west the college lies back
to back with the gloomy and austere courts of Lincoln.
There is no sense of space, of leisureliness, of ornament
about the place ; it rather looks like a fortress of study.

You enter the first court by a gateway under a
tower. The interior of the buildings is still more
sombre, with the smoke-stained walls and gables of
friable stone. The Hall is on the south side, a lofty,
dark-panelled place, with some good portraits. Beyond the Hall on the first floor is the Common-room,
whither the Fellows adjourn after Hall, and which by
day answers the purpose of a club-room. This is also
an ample panelled chamber, with an air about it of
grave and solid comfort.

The further court, to the south, which is entered
by a flagged arched passage under the southern wing
of the first court, is an irregular place, having been

of late years considerably extended. The Chapel at
once attracts the eye. It is a Renaissance building, of
the same crumbling Headington stone, with broad
classical pilasters, and windows of a clumsy Gothic
tracery. The designer appears to have wished the
tone to be classical, with a Gothic flavour. The very
incongruity has a certain sober charm. A beautiful
Renaissance porch admits to the ante-chapel; a fine
classical screen of dark wood, with large smooth
columns, supports an organ, into the carved woodwork
of which are wrought gilded swans and peacocks.
There is a noble classical western window, under
which is set the memorial to Pater. This is not
wholly satisfactory, looking like a little tray of coins.
It has four medallions—Leonardo, Michel Angelo,
Dante, and Plato—with a fifth in the centre containing
a bas-relief of Pater's head; but the expression is irrit-
able and the chin is exaggeratedly protruded. The
mottoes above and below, in uncial Greek, are beautiful
and appropriate: ΩC · ΦΙΛΟCΟΦΙΑS · ΟΥCΗC · ΤΗC ·
ΜΕΓΙCΤΗC · ΜΟΥCΙΚΗC (since philosophy is the
greatest music) above; and ΟCΑ · ΕCΤΙΝ · ΑΛΗΘΗ ·
ΟCΑ · CΕΜΝΑ · ΟCΑ · ΑΓΑΘΑ below (whatsoever
things are true, whatsoever things are holy, whatsoever
things are pure).

The interior of the chapel has the same simple
gravity. There is a plain marble reredos; the stall-
work is Jacobean of dark wood, the heavy cornice
and the balls which serve for poppy-heads being con-
spicuous. There is a great brazen chandelier and a
noble eagle lectern. The roof, taken from the destroyed
chapel of St. Mary's College, which stood on the site
now occupied by Frewin Hall, is of a rich Gothic,
brightly painted. The east window is a fine piece of
classical glass, but there are some poor ecclesiastical

windows at the side; of which it may be recorded that
when the question of replacing them was mooted, Pater
said that he would not have them removed, as they
provided a document of taste. The velvet cushions,
the tall prayer-books give a dignified eighteenth-
century air to the whole.

There is something in these classical Oxford chapels
which lends a curious and distinct savour to the offices
of religion. It has been said that Gothic represents
the aspiration of man to God, classical architecture the
tabernacling of God with men. There is a species of
truth in the statement. But it would perhaps be truer
to say that in Gothic one sees the uncultivated instinct
for beauty feeling its way out of barbarism into a
certain ecclesiastical and traditional grace. But the
classical enshrinement of religious worship seems to
hint at a desire to bring the older and loftier triumphs
of the human mind, the Greek and Roman spirit, into
the service of the sanctuary. Gothic seems to depict
the untutored spirit of man, nurtured on nature and
religion, working out a wild and native grace in intricacy of tracery and ornament. But the classical
setting brings with it a sober and settled air, a wider
and larger range of human interests, a certain
antiquity of mental culture.

Pater's own rooms are approached by a staircase in
the south-east corner of the first court, which leads
to a little thick-walled panelled parlour, now white,
then painted a delicate yellow, with black doors; an
old-fashioned scroll round the mantelpiece was picked
out in gold. The deeply recessed oriel window
looks out upon the Radcliffe. Some trace of Pater's
dainty ways lingers in the pretty and fantastic ironwork of the doors, brought by him from Brittany.
The room was always furnished with a certain

B

seemly austerity and simplicity, never crowded with ornament. His only luxury was a bowl of dried rose-leaves. He had little desire to possess intrinsically valuable objects, and a few engravings served rather to remind him of the noble originals than to represent them. Thus there exists, now in the possession of the Principal of Brasenose, a little tray of copies of beautiful Greek coins, bearing large heads with smooth and liberal curves, and other dainty devices, on which Pater loved to feast his eyes. Mr. Humphry Ward writes :—

"I well remember my first visit to his rooms—small, freshly painted in greenish white, and hung with three or four line-engravings. All dons had line-engravings then, but they were all after Raphael. Pater had something more character-istic : the 'Three Fates,' attributed to M. Angelo ; a head after Correggio ; and I think something of Ingres—a new name to Oxford ! The clean, clear table, the stained border round the matting and Eastern carpet, and the scanty, bright chintz curtains, were a novelty and a contrast to the oaken respectability and heaviness of all other dons' rooms at that day. The effect was in keeping with his own clear-cut view of life, and made, in a small way, 'the colours freshen on this threadbare world.'"

But there was no luxury, no sumptuousness, no seductiveness of comfort about his surroundings. That might be left to those who misinterpreted him. To the serious student, pleasure and joy must always have a certain bracing austerity ; might be sipped, perhaps, held up to the light, dwelt upon, but not plunged into nor rioted upon.

Out of the little panelled sitting-room opened a door, which led into a narrow passage full of cupboards, and admitted the occupant, by a low, ancient, stone-framed, Gothic doorway, into a tiny slip of a bedroom, only a

few feet wide. At one end a little window looked out
into the court ; at the other end was an odd projection,
like a couple of steps, above the floor, forming the roof
of the small cramped staircase below. Considerations
of space were so exacting that the head of the bed had
to rest, without legs, on the projection. The rest of
the room only just admitted a chest of drawers and
a simple toilet apparatus. In this miniature room
Pater slept through the whole of his Oxford days. He
went to bed early, but in later days was an indifferent
sleeper, and to beguile the time before he could close
his eyes, worked slowly through the *Dictionary of
National Biography*, volume by volume. He had
frequent opportunities of changing these rooms for
a better set ; but partly from economy, and partly from
the extreme simplicity which characterised him, he preferred to stay. It is indeed almost inconceivable that
a man engaged on literary work requiring such delicate
concentration, should have lived so contentedly in rooms
of such narrow resources. The little sitting-room gave
straight upon the free air of the open passage. On a
small square table his meals would be spread. His
outer door was always open ; he was always accessible,
never seemed to be interrupted by any visitor, was
never impatient, always courteous and deferential ;
rising from a little round table near the fire, in the
middle of the most complicated sentence, the most
elaborate piece of word-construction.

His habits were marked by the same ascetic simplicity. He never took afternoon tea, he never smoked.
His meals were plain to austerity. But he took great
pains with the little entertainments he gave, ordering
every item and writing the menu-cards himself. The
morning, he used to say, was the time for creation,
the afternoon for correction. He did very little work

in the evening. His habits were absolutely regular;
few days were without their tale of quiet study. He
concerned himself very little with college matters,
though he held various college offices; he was at one
time Tutor and at the end of his life Dean. He lectured
to the passmen, and later gave public lectures, of which
the volume *Plato and Platonism* was the fruit. One
of his friends remembers attending these lectures : a
number of undergraduates arrived, spread out their
notebooks and prepared to take notes ; but the attempt
was soon abandoned, the lecturer reading, slowly and
continuously, in a soft mellow voice, one carefully
turned phrase after another. Mr. Humphry Ward
writes :—

"Then, I suppose about May 1867, came his first lectures.
Only six or eight Brasenose men were then reading for
classical Greats ; the system of 'combined' college lectures,
to which afterwards Pater owed the large audiences that came
to hear him on Plato, was not yet invented. We were six
men, some novices, some dull, all quite unprepared for Pater.
He sat down and began—it was the 'History of Philosophy.'
We expected the old formulæ about Thales, and some refer-
ences to Aristotle that we could take down in our books and
use for the Schools. It was nothing of the kind. It was a
quickly delivered discourse, rather Comtian, on the Dogmatic
and Historical methods : quite new to me, and worse than
new to some others. I remember, as we went out, a senior
man, F——, who used to amaze us by his ready translations of
Thucydides in 'Mods' lectures, and who passed as extremely
clever—as he was in that line—F. threw down his note-book
with the cry, 'No more of that for me : if Greats mean *that*,
I'll cut 'em !' (as he wisely did)."

Among Pater's chief friends were, in early days, Pro-
fessor Ingram Bywater, his contemporary at Queen's,
Dr. Edward Caird, now Master of Balliol, Professor
Nettleship, Mr. W. W. Capes, tutor of Queen's; but

his closest friend and lifelong companion was Mr.
C. L. Shadwell, then of Christ Church, now Provost of
Oriel, who had been for a short time his private pupil.
Pater often travelled in his company, and on Pater's
death he undertook to act as his literary executor, a task
which he has fulfilled with a rare loyalty and discretion.

The friends of a somewhat later date were Mark
Pattison, the Rector of Lincoln; Bishop Creighton,
then a Fellow of Merton; the present Provost of
Worcester, Dr. Daniel, and Mrs. Daniel; Mr. Humphry
Ward, a Fellow of Brasenose, and his future wife,
Miss Mary Arnold; Mr. Warren, now President of
Magdalen; of the larger world, Mr. Swinburne, who
often visited Oxford, Dr. Appleton, then editor of the
Academy, Mr. Basil Champneys, and Mr. Edmund
Gosse; in more recent days Mr. Douglas Ainslie,
Mr. Arthur Symons, and Mr. Lionel Johnson; but
in later years Pater was perhaps more often cheered
and encouraged by the devoted companionship of
Dr. F. W. Bussell, now Vice-Principal of Brasenose,
than by any other of his friendships.

But, though one may enumerate his closer friends,
Pater did not make friends easily, unless he was
met with a certain simple candour and ready sympathy; what he valued was a quiet domestic companionship, in which he could talk easily of what was
in his mind. To those that were without he showed
a certain suave and amiable deference; and even to
his intimates he was often reserved, baffling, and mysterious, from a deep-seated reticence and reserve.

When Pater was settled at Brasenose, he took a
house, No. 2 Bradmore Road, in Norham Gardens,
which gave him opportunities for simple hospitality
and the easy domestic background that he loved.
He liked to have friends to stay quietly with him,

and always manifested an extreme solicitude about
the comfort of his guests down to the smallest details,
planning the days that they spent with him so
that they should be entertained and amused. "Are
you comfortable?" was a question, uttered with the
delicate and deliberate precision of pronunciation, that
was constantly on his lips. But the entertaining
of guests tired him, partly because it interfered
with the simple and leisurely routine of the day,
and partly because, with his scrupulous considerateness,
it put a great strain on his sympathy. He could not
pursue his usual habits and leave his guests to amuse
themselves; he was always conscious that they were
in the house, and felt the responsibility for their
comfort and amusement very deeply.

To give an impression of him in those early days, I
will quote Mr. Ward's words:—

"When I entered Brasenose as a freshman-scholar in
October, 1864, W. H. Pater was junior Fellow. I did not
make his acquaintance till long afterwards, but from the first
I was struck with his appearance, his high, rather receding
forehead; his bright eyes, placed near together, his face clean-
shaven except for a short moustache (this was rare in those
days), his slight stoop, and his quick walk with a curious swing
of the shoulders. As I got to know senior men, especially
of other colleges, I gradually became conscious that Pater was
already vaguely celebrated in the University. He was supposed to have a new and daring philosophy of his own, and a
wonderful gift of style, owing his Fellowship to these two, for
he was no scholar, as the Universities understand the word."

That Pater was no scholar, in the technical sense of
the word, is true enough; but he answered rather to
Lord Macaulay's definition of a scholar, as one who
read Plato with his feet on the fender. He was not
at any time a great reader or a profound student;

he was on the look-out for quality rather than for
definite facts. He was very fastidious about the
style even of authors whose matter and treatment
he admired. "I admire Poe's originality and imagination," he once said, "but I cannot read him in the
original. He is so rough; I read him in Baude-
laire's translation." Indeed he read less and less as
time went on; in later years, apart from reading under-
taken for definite purposes, he concentrated himself
more and more upon a few great books, such as Plato
and the Bible, which he often read in the Vulgate; he
made no attempt at any time to keep abreast of the
literature of the day.

Pater regarded his Oxford life primarily as a life of
quiet literary study; this was his chief object; he had
a strong natural dislike of responsibility; he did not
consider himself a professional educator, though he
thought it a plain duty to give encouragement and sympathy in intellectual things to any students who desired
or needed direction. But he did not conceive that
there ought to be any question of disciplinary training
or coercion in the matter; to those who required help,
he gave it eagerly, patiently, generously; but he
never thought of himself as a species of schoolmaster,
whose business it was to make men work; on the
other hand he realised his personal responsibility to
the full. He was always ready to give advice about
work, about the choice of a profession, and above all
laboured to clear away the scruples of men who had
intended to enter the ministry of the church, and
found themselves doubtful of their vocation. He had
a special sympathy for the ecclesiastical life, and was
anxious to remove any obstacles, to resolve any doubts,
which young men are so liable to encounter in their
undergraduate days.

As Dr. Bussell, in a Memorial Sermon preached in Brasenose Chapel after Pater's death, finely said, we may see in Pater

"a pattern of the student life, an example of the mind which feels its own responsibilities, which holds and will use the key of knowledge ; severely critical of itself and its own performances ; genially tolerant of others ; keenly appreciating their merit ; a modest and indulgent censor ; a sympathetic adviser."

His attitude towards younger men was always serious and kindly, but he never tried to exert influence, or to seek the society of those whose views he felt to be antipathetic. That a man should be ardently disposed to athletic pursuits was no obstacle to Pater's friendship, though he was himself entirely averse to games ; it rather constituted an additional reason for admiring one with whom he felt otherwise in sympathy, though it was no passport to his favour. He took no part in questions of discipline, which at Brasenose are entirely in the hands of a single officer ; indeed it is recorded that on the only occasion when he was called upon to assist in quelling an outbreak of rowdyism, he contrived to turn a hose, intended to quench a bonfire, into the window of an undergraduate's bedroom, to whom he had afterwards to give leave to sleep out of college in consequence of the condition of his rooms.

Besides delivering lectures, it was a chief part of Pater's work to look over and criticise the essays of his pupils. He spent a great deal of pains on the essays submitted to him ; he seldom set subjects, but required that a man should choose a subject in which he was interested. It is usual for a lecturer to have an essay read aloud to him, and to make what criticisms he

can, as they arise in his mind, without previous preparation. But Pater had the essays shown up to him,
scrutinised them carefully, even pencilling comments
upon the page; and then, in an interview, he gave
careful verdicts as to style and arrangement, and
made many effective and practical suggestions. Mr.
Humphry Ward says, "He was severe on confusions
of thought, and still more so on any kind of rhetoric.
An emphatic word or epithet was sure to be under-
scored, and the absolutely right phrase suggested."
Pater always followed a precise ritual on these occasions. He always appeared, whatever he might be
doing, to be entirely unoccupied; he would vacate
his only arm-chair and instal the pupil in it; and then
going to the window, he would take his place on the
window-seat and say, "Well, let us see what this is
all about."

Though his own literary bent was so clearly defined,
he never had the least idea of forming a school of
writers on the model of his own style; all such direct
influences were distasteful to him; he merely aimed
at giving advice which should result in the attainment
of the most lucid and individual statement possible.
He had no sort of desire to be a master or a leader,
or to direct disciples on any but the old and traditional lines. His principle indeed was the Socratic
ideal—"to encourage young men to take an interest
in themselves."

He would sometimes ask a student to join him
in the vacation, which must have been a severe tax on
one so independent and fond of seclusion as Pater,
when he would coach him and walk with him. At the
same time, says one of those who came within his
circle in later days, it was felt that his relations with
younger men were guided more by a sense of duty than

by instinct. He was like Telemachus, "decent not to fail in offices of tenderness." He was careful, says the same friend, to write and inquire about one's interests and one's progress. But it was clear that he was in a way self-centred, that he *depended* on no one, but lived in a world of his own, working out his own thoughts with a firm concentration, and that though he was endlessly kind and absolutely faithful, yet that few made any vital difference to him. He was a steady friend, and always responsive to the charm of youth, of sympathy, of intellectual interest. But even those who were brought into close contact with him were apt to feel that far down in his nature lurked a certain untamed scepticism, a suspension of mind, that lay deeper than his hopes and even than his beliefs. But it was impossible to doubt his real tenderness of heart, his fellow-feeling, his goodness.

Mr. Ward, who spent part of a summer vacation at this time in Pater's company, writes :—

"The month at Sidmouth made us rather intimate, and afterwards I often walked and lunched with Pater at Oxford. He had begun to publish then : the articles on 'Coleridge' and 'Winckelmann' in the *Westminster Review* had appeared, and had made a great sensation in the University. Unfamiliar with Goethe at first-hand, and with the French romantics such as Théophile Gautier, the men of about my standing had their first revelation of the neo-Cyrenaic philosophy and of the theory of Art for Art, in these papers. None the less, even those of us who were most attracted by them, and men like myself to whom Pater was personally very kind, found *intimacy* with him very difficult. He could be tremendously interesting in talk ; his phrases, his point of view, were original and always stimulating ; but you never felt that he was quite at one with you in habits, feelings, preferences. His inner world was not that of any one else at Oxford."

CHAPTER II

EARLY WRITINGS

I HAVE thought it best in this study of a life marked by so few external events, to follow as far as possible the chronological order of Pater's writings, for this reason : that though he revealed in conversation and social intercourse scarcely anything of the workings and the progress of his mind, yet his writings constitute a remarkable self-revelation of a character of curious intensity and depth, within certain defined limits.

After disentangling himself from metaphysical speculations, after what may be called his artistic conversion, which dates from his first journey to Italy, he threw himself with intense concentration into the task of developing his power of expression. Thus his first deliberate work is a species of manifesto, an enunciation of the principles with which he began his artistic pilgrimage.

The interest of the study "Winckelmann" is very great. It has been made the subject of a myth, the legend being that it was written while Pater was a boy at school. This statement, which is wholly without foundation, is only worth mentioning in order that it may be contradicted. The origin of the story is probably to be found in the desire to make Pater's boyhood prophetic of his later interests ; but the study

was as a matter of fact written in 1866. It appeared
in January 1867, in the *Westminster Review.*

There is a charm about the early work of writers
whose style is strongly individual. Sometimes these
early attempts are tentative and unequal, as if the
writer had not yet settled down to a deliberate style;
they bear traces of the effect of other favourite styles.
The curtain seems to rise, so to speak, jerkily, and to
reveal the performer by glimpses; but in the case of
the "Winckelmann" the curtain goes up tranquilly
and evenly, and the real Pater steps quietly upon
the stage.

The style in which "Winckelmann" is written is a
formed style; it contains all the characteristics which
give Pater his unique distinction. It is closely and
elaborately packed; the sentences have the long
stately cadences; the epithets have the *soigneux*
flavour; and it is full, too, of those delicate and suggestive passages, where a beautiful image is hinted,
with a severe economy of art, rather than worked out in
the Ruskinian fashion. There is, too, a rigid suppression of the ornamental; it is like gold from which the
encompassing gravel has been washed. But it has also
a passion, a glow, which is somewhat in contrast to a
certain sense of weariness that creeps into some of the
later work. It is youthful, ardent, indiscreet. But
for all that it is accurately proportioned and mature.
It shows the power, which is very characteristic of
Pater, of condensing an exact knowledge of detail into
a few paragraphs, retaining what is salient and illuminating, and giving the effect of careful selection.

It is plain, in the "Winckelmann," that the writer
had been hitherto occupied in somewhat experimental
researches; but here he seems to have found his own
point of view in a moment, and to have suddenly appre-

hended his attitude to the world. It is as when a carrier-pigeon released from its prison beats round and round, determining by some mysterious instinct the direction of its home ; and at lasts sweeps off, without doubt or hesitation, with steady strokes on the chosen path.

Winckelmann was one who, after a dark and poverty-stricken youth, of mental and indeed physical starvation, became aware of the perfect beauty of Greek art, and renounced all study but that of the literature of the arts, till he became " consummate, tranquil, withdrawn into the region of ideals, yet retaining colour from the incidents of a passionate intellectual life." He renounced his metaphysical and legal studies, in which he had made progress. He joined the Church of Rome, to gain the patronage of the Saxon Court ; and finally transferred himself to Rome, where he wrote his *History of Ancient Art.* He lived a life of severe simplicity, absorbed entirely in intellectual and artistic study, his only connection with the world in which he lived being a series of romantic and almost passionate friendships. His end was tragic ; for he was murdered by a fellow-traveller at Trieste for the sake of some gold medals which he had received at Vienna. Goethe, whose intellectual ideal had been deeply affected by Winckelmann's writings, was awaiting his arrival at Leipsic with intense enthusiasm, but was not destined ever to see him.

Such was the figure that appealed so strongly to Pater's mind ; and perhaps the chief interest of the essay is the strong autobiographical element that appears in it. Pater saw in Winckelmann a type of himself, of his own intellectual struggles, of his own conversion to the influence of art. After a confused and blinded youth, self-contained and meagrely

nourished, Winckelmann had struck out, without
hesitation or uneasy lingering, on his path among the
stars. It is impossible not to feel in many passages
that Pater is reading his own soul-history into that
of his hero.

"It is easy," he writes, "to indulge the commonplace metaphysical instinct. But a taste for metaphysics may be one
of those things which we must renounce, if we mean to mould
our lives to artistic perfection. Philosophy serves culture,
not by the fancied gift of absolute or transcendental knowledge, but by suggesting questions which help one to detect
the passion, and strangeness, and dramatic contrasts of life."

And again :—

"Certainly, for us of the modern world, with its conflicting
claims, its entangled interests, distracted by so many sorrows,
so many preoccupations, so bewildering an experience, the
problem of unity with ourselves, in blitheness and repose, is
far harder than it was for the Greek within the simple terms
of antique life. . . . The pure instinct of self-culture cares not so
much to reap all that these forms of culture can give, as to
find in them its own strength. The demand of the intellect
is to feel itself alive. It must see into the laws, the operation,
the intellectual reward of every divided form of culture ;
but only that it may measure the relation between itself and
them. It struggles with those forms till its secret is won from
each, and then lets each fall back into its place, in the supreme,
artistic view of life. With a kind of passionate coldness, such
natures rejoice to be away from and past their former selves."

And once again :—

"On a sudden the imagination feels itself free. How
facile and direct, it seems to say, is this life of the senses and
the understanding, when once we have apprehended it ! Here,
surely, is the more liberal life we have been seeking so long,
so near to us all the while. How mistaken and roundabout
have been our efforts to reach it by mystic passion, and

monastic reverie ; how they have deflowered the flesh ; how
little they have emancipated us ! "

An eager intensity of feeling thrills through these
impassioned sentences. One feels instinctively that
the writer of these words, after years of blind and
mute movements, like the worm in the cocoon, had
suddenly broken free, and had seen his creased and
folded wings expand and glitter in the sun.   Art,
friendship, perception, emotion, that was the true
life he had been desiring so long; and yet, after all,
what an inner life it was to be ! There was no impulse
to fling himself into the current of the world, to taste
the life of cities, where the social eddy spun swift
and strong ; he was to be austere, self-centred, silent
still.   Only in seclusion was he to utter his impassioned dreams in a congenial ear.   " Blitheness and
repose ! " these were to be the keynotes of the new
life ; a clear-sighted mastery of intellectual problems,
a joyful perception of the beauties of art, a critical
attitude, that was to be able to distinguish by practised
insight what was perfect and permanent from what
was merely bold and temporary. And so, light of
heart, his imagination revelling at the thought of all
the realms of beauty it was to traverse, undimmed
and radiant, the dumb and darkened past providing
the contrast needed to bring out the brightness and
the hope of what lay before, Pater set out upon his
pilgrimage. And yet there is a shadow. As he writes
in one of the most pathetic sentences, in one of his
later and most tender sketches, of just such another
pilgrimage, " Could he have foreseen the weariness of
the way ! "

The years began to pass slowly and quietly. Pater
performed his tale of prescribed work, and gave himself over to leisurely study and meditation.   He was

not averse to social pleasures in these days, and began
to make congenial acquaintances, among whom he gained
a reputation as a brilliant and paradoxical talker.   He
fed his sense of beauty by frequent visits to Italy,
though he never gained more than a superficial acquaintance either with Italian art or modern Italian life.
He was in this matter always an eclectic, following his
own preferences and guided by his prejudices.   He had
little catholicity of view, and seldom studied the work
of artists with whom he did not feel himself at once in
sympathy.   His travels were rather a diligent storing
of beautiful impressions.   He wrote to Mr. Edmund
Gosse in 1877, of a visit to Azay-le-Rideau :—

"We find always great pleasure in adding to our experiences of these French places, and return always a little tired,
indeed, but with our minds pleasantly full of memories of
stained glass, old tapestries and new flowers."

Pater certainly showed no undue haste to garner the
harvest of the brain in these years.   He was studying,
enjoying, meditating.   He wrote at the rate of a short
essay or two a year.   The essay of 1868 on " Aesthetic
Poetry " was suppressed for twenty-one years.   In 1869
he wrote the " Notes on Leonardo da Vinci," one of the
most elaborate and characteristic of his writings.   In
1870 it was " A Fragment on Sandro Botticelli."   In
1871 it was " Pico della Mirandola " and the " Poetry
of Michelangelo."   All these appeared in the *Fortnightly Review*.   And then in 1873 he produced his first
book, *Studies in the History of the Renaissance*, in which
he included, together with those studies which had pre-
viously been published, a Preface and a "Conclusion,"
both of which are of deep significance in studying the
course of Pater's mental development, and three other
essays : "Aucassin and Nicolette " (in later editions

named "Two Early French Stories,"), "Luca della
Robbia," and "Joachim du Bellay." To these, in the
third edition of the *Studies* (1888), was added "The
School of Giorgione," which had appeared in the *Fortnightly Review* for October 1877 ; while in the second
edition of the book, which came out in the same year
(1877), the "Conclusion" was omitted, but re-appeared
with slight modifications in the third edition.

The essay on "Aesthetic Poetry" eventually appeared, as we have said, in 1889 in *Appreciations*, but
it was again omitted in the second edition of that
volume (1890), and does not appear in the complete
issue of his works.

I do not know what it was that made Pater withdraw the essay on "Aesthetic Poetry," written in 1868,
from the later issue of *Appreciations*. Probably some
unfavourable or wounding criticism, expressing a belief
that he was closer to these exotic fancies than he knew
himself to be. It is a strange and somewhat dreamy
composition, rather a mystical meditation upon a
phase of thought than a disentangling of precise
principles. He takes William Morris's *Defence of
Guenevere* as a text, saying that "the poem which gives
its name to the volume is a thing tormented and awry
with passion . . . and the accent falls in strange, unwonted places with the effect of a great cry." He says
that the secret of the enjoyment of this new poetry,
with the artificial, earthly paradise that it creates, is
"that inversion of home-sickness known to some, that
incurable thirst for the sense of escape, which no actual
form of life satisfies, no poetry even, if it be merely
simple and spontaneous." He compares the movement
with the development of mystical religious literature,
and defines the dangerous emotionalism of the monastic
form of life, when adopted by persons of strongly sen-

suous temperament, saying that such natures learn
from religion "the art of directing towards an unseen object sentiments whose natural direction is towards objects of sense." "Here, under this strange
complex of conditions, as in some medicated air, exotic
flowers of sentiment expand, among people of a remote
and unaccustomed beauty, somnambulistic, frail, andro-
gynous, the light almost shining through them."

One cannot help feeling that the above sentence
may be the very passage, from the air of strange
passion which stirs in it, for which the essay was
condemned. Or again the following sentence: "He
(Morris) has diffused through 'King Arthur's Tomb'
the maddening white glare of the sun, and tyranny of
the moon, not tender and far-off, but close down—the
sorcerer's moon, large and feverish. The colouring is
intricate and delirious, as of 'scarlet lilies.' The
influence of summer is like a poison in one's blood,
with a sudden bewildered sickening of life and all
things." There is indeed a certain disorder of the
sense in this passage, the hint of a dangerous mood
which seems to grasp after strange delights and evil
secrets, in a reckless and haunted twilight. It is a
veritable *fleur du mal*; and Pater, with his strong
instinct for restraint and austerity of expression, probably felt that he was thus setting a perilous example
of over-sensuous imagery, and an exotic lusciousness
of thought.

He goes on to say that in this poetry, life seems to
break from conventional things, and to realise experience, pleasure, and pain alike, as new and startling
things for which no poetry, no tradition, no usage had
prepared it. "Everywhere there is an impression of
surprise, as of people first waking from the golden age,
at fire, snow, wine, the touch of water as one swims,

the salt taste of the sea. And this simplicity at first
hand is a strange contrast to the sought-out simplicity
of Wordsworth. Desire here is towards the body of
nature for its own sake, not because a soul is divined
through it." He shows that even Morris's classical
poems, such as *Jason* and the *Earthly Paradise*, are
filled and saturated with the medieval spirit; for
it will be remembered that though the setting of
the *Earthly Paradise* is primarily medieval, yet the
point of the poem is that we are supposed to be
brought into contact with "a reserved fragment of
Greece, which by some divine good fortune lingers on
in the western sea into the Middle Age." The pagan
element, he points out, is "the continual suggestion,
pensive or passionate, of the shortness of life," contrasting with the natural unspoiled joy in the beauty of
the world.

Early as the essay is, in the date of its composition,
one feels that Pater, by omitting it from later editions,
was deliberately retracing his steps, conscious that he
had turned aside, in writing it, into a bypath of the
spirit, and away from the more sober and serious ideal
of his life. Its strange beauty is undeniable; but in
its omission we see, as it were, a warning hand held
up, indicating that not in this luxurious gloom, this
enervating atmosphere, are the true ends of the spirit
to be attained.

The Studies in the History of the Renaissance deserve
close attention, in the first place for themselves, because
of the elaborateness of the art displayed, the critical
subtlety with which typical qualities are seized and interpreted. As the bee ranges over flowers at will, and
gathers a tiny draught of honey from each, which, though
appropriated, secreted, and reproduced, still bears the
flavour of the particular flower, whether of the garden

violet or the wild heather-bell, from which it was drawn, so these essays exhibit each a characteristic savour of the art or the figure which furnished them. They are no shallow or facile impressions, but bear the marks of resolute compression and fine selection. But they are not mere forms reflected in the mirror of a perceptive mind. They are in the truest sense symbolical, charged to the brim with the personality of the writer, and thus to be ranged with creative rather than critical art. Those who cannot see with Pater's eyes may look in vain, in the writings or the pictures of which he speaks, for the mysterious suggestiveness of line and colour which he discerns in them. They have suffered in passing through the medium of his perception, like the bones of the drowned king, "a sea-change into something rich and strange"; they are like the face which he describes, into which the soul with all its maladies had passed. It is hardly for us to estimate the ethical significance of the attitude revealed. It must suffice to say that in the hands of Pater these pictures out of the past have been transmuted by a secret and deep current of emotion into something behind and beyond the outer form. They are charged with dreams.

And in the second place they reveal, perhaps, the sincerest emotions of a mind at its freshest and strongest. No considerations of prudence or discretion influenced his thought. Few writers perhaps preserve, through fame and misunderstanding alike, so consistent, so individual an attitude as Pater. But it must also be borne in mind that he was deeply sensitive, and though he was deliberately and instinctively sincere in all his work, yet in his later writings one feels that criticism and even misrepresentation had an effect upon him. He realised that there were certain veins of thought that were not convenient;

that the frank enunciation of principles evoked impatience and even suspicion in the sturdy and breezy English mind. He held on his way indeed, though with a certain sadness. But there is no touch of that outer sadness in these first delicate and fanciful creations; the sadness that breathes through them is the inner sadness, the veiled melancholy that makes her sovereign shrine in the very temple of delight. Here, too, may be seen the impassioned joy that is born of the shock of exquisite impressions coming home to a nature that is widening and deepening every hour.

The preface of the book strikes a firm note of personality. Pater is here seen to be in strong revolt against the synthetic school of art-criticism. The business of the aesthetic critic, he declares with solemn earnestness, is not to attempt a definition of abstract beauty, but to realise the relativity of beauty, and to discern the quality, the virtue, of the best art of a writer or an artist. He explains too his principle of selection, namely that while the interest of the Renaissance is centred in Italy, its outer ripples, so to speak, must be studied in French poetry as well as in the later German manifestations of the same spirit.

There is an interesting passage, in the recent memoir of Lady Dilke, about Pater's *Renaissance*. It will be remembered that when the book appeared she was the wife of Mark Pattison. She was then much engaged in the practice of art-criticism, and reviewed the book with some severity, as lacking in scientific exactness and in historical perspective. She thought that Pater had isolated the movement from its natural origins, and complained that he had treated the Renaissance as "an air-plant, independent of the ordinary sources of nourishment . . . a sentimental revolution having no

relation to the actual conditions of the world." This
criticism has a certain truth in it, and gains interest
from the fact that it probably to a certain extent
represents the mature judgment of Pattison himself.
But it is based on a misconception of the scope of the
book, and is sufficiently rebutted by the modest title
of the volume, *Studies in the History of the Renaissance.*
The book, indeed, lays no claim to be an exhaustive
treatment of the movement.   It is only a poetical and
suggestive interpretation of certain brilliant episodes,
springing from deeper causes which Pater made no
attempt to indicate.

In the first essay, "Aucassin and Nicolette," he
points out that the sweetness of the Renaissance is
not only derived from the classical world, but from
the native outpouring of the spirit which showed itself
in ecclesiastical art and in native French poetry, and
which prompted and prepared the way for the enthusiastic return to classical art.

In "Pico della Mirandola" he traces the attempt to
reconcile the principles of Christianity with the religion of ancient Greece, not by any historical or philosophical method, but by allegorical interpretation, in
the spirit of that "generous belief that nothing which
had ever interested the human mind could wholly lose
its vitality."   He dwells with wistful delight upon the
figure of this graceful and precocious scholar, Pico,
"Earl of Mirandola, and a great Lord of Italy"—Pico,
nurtured in the law, but restless and athirst, with the
eager and uncritical zest of the time, for philosophy,
for language, for religion, working, fitfully and brilliantly, in the hope that some solution would be found
to satisfy the yearnings of the soul, some marvellous
secret, which would in a moment gratify and harmonise
all curious and warring impulses.   Pico, beloved of

women, seemly and gracious of mien, dying of fever at so early an age, and lying down for his last rest in the grave habit of the Dominicans, mystical, ardent, weary with the weariness that comes of so swift and perilous a pilgrimage, is a type of beauty shadowed by doom, mortality undimmed by age or disease, that appealed with passionate force to Pater's mind.

In the essay on "Sandro Botticelli" he touches on the meditative subtlety, the visionary melancholy, of the painter, "the peculiar sentiment with which he infuses his profane and sacred persons, comely, and in a certain sense like angels, but with a sense of displacement or loss about them — the wistfulness of exiles, conscious of a passion and energy greater than any known issue of them explains, which runs through all his varied work with a sentiment of ineffable melancholy." He traces the strange mixture of idealism and realism which transfuses Botticelli's pictures, his men and women, "clothed sometimes by passion with a character of loveliness and energy, but saddened perpetually by the shadow upon them of the great things from which they shrink. His morality is all sympathy." He confesses frankly that Botticelli displays an incomplete grasp of the resources of art; but he indicates with subtle perception the haunted and wistful spirit of the artist.

In the "Luca della Robbia" Pater traces very skilfully the attempt made to unite the pleasure derivable from sculpture with the homely art of pottery, the old-world modesty and seriousness and simplicity which put out its strength to adorn and cultivate daily household life; and he shows, too, the exquisite *intimité* and the originality of the man, which is so rarely exhibited in the white abstract art of sculpture.

The *motif* of the "Poetry of Michelangelo" is best

summed up in the words which Pater uses as a re-
current phrase : *ex forti dulcedo*—out of the strong
came forth sweetness. He says :—

"The interest of Michelangelo's poems is that they make
us spectators of this struggle ; the struggle of a strong nature
to adorn and attune itself ; the struggle of a desolating
passion, which yearns to be resigned and sweet and pensive,
as Dante's was."

The essay beautifully contrasts the extremes of that
volcanic nature, the man who, as Raphael said, walked
the streets of Rome like an executioner, and who yet,
at the other end of the scale, could conceive and bring
to perfection the exquisite sweetness, the almost over-
composed dignity, of the great *Pietà*. The essay
abounds in subtle and delicate characterisation of the
manifestations of that desirous, rugged, uncomforted
nature. Thus, in speaking of the four symbolical
figures, *Night, Day, The Twilight, The Dawn*, which adorn
the sacristy of San Lorenzo, Pater says that the names
assigned them are far too precise.—

"They concentrate and express, less by way of definite
conceptions than by the touches, the promptings of a piece of
music, all those vague fancies, misgivings, presentiments,
which shift and mix and define themselves and fade again,
whenever the thoughts try to fix themselves with sincerity on
the conditions and surroundings of the disembodied spirit. I
suppose no one would come to the sacristy of San Lorenzo for
consolation ; for seriousness, for solemnity, for dignity of impression, perhaps, but not for consolation. It is a place neither
of terrible nor consoling thoughts, but of vague and wistful
speculation."

Perhaps it may be said that in this essay Pater reveals an over-subtlety of conception in his desire to

substantiate the contrast. There was an essential unity of character, of aim, about Michelangelo ; and the contrasts are merely the same intensity of mood working in different regions, not a difference of mood. The chief value of the essay lies in its lyrical fervour, in the poetical and suggestive things that are said by the way.

The essay on "Leonardo da Vinci" is certainly the most brilliant of all the essays, and contains elaborate passages which, for meditative sublimity and exquisite phrasing, Pater never surpassed. The fitful, mysterious, beauty-haunted nature of Leonardo, the stream of his life broken into such various channels, his absorption, his remoteness, passing "unmoved through the most tragic events, overwhelming his country and friends, like one who comes across them by chance on some secret errand"—all this had a potent attraction for Pater. The essay is a wonderful piece of constructive skill, interweaving as it does all the salient features of the "legend" of Vasari with a perfect illustrative felicity. But it is in the descriptive passages that Pater touches the extreme of skill, as for instance in his description of the sea-shore of the Saint Anne, "that delicate place, where the wind passes like the hand of some fine etcher over the surface, and the untorn shells are lying thick upon the sand, and the tops of the rocks, to which the waves never rise, are green with grass, grown fine as hair. It is the landscape, not of dreams or of fancy, but of places far withdrawn, and hours selected from a thousand with a miracle of *finesse*. Through Leonardo's strange veil of sight things reach him so ; in no ordinary night or day, but as in faint light of eclipse, or in some brief interval of falling rain at daybreak, or through deep water."

Though the celebrated passage which describes " La

Gioconda" has been abundantly quoted, it may here be given in full :—

"The presence that thus rose so strangely beside the waters, is expressive of what in the ways of a thousand years men had come to desire. Hers is the head upon which all 'the ends of the world are come,' and the eyelids are a little weary. It is a beauty wrought out from within upon the flesh, the deposit, little cell by cell, of strange thoughts and fantastic reveries and exquisite passions. Set it for a moment beside one of those white Greek goddesses or beautiful women of antiquity, and how would they be troubled by this beauty, into which the soul with all its maladies has passed ! All the thoughts and experience of the world have etched and moulded there, in that which they have of power to refine and make expressive the outward form, the animalism of Greece, the lust of Rome, the reverie of the middle age with its spiritual ambition and imaginative loves, the return of the Pagan world, the sins of the Borgias. She is older than the rocks among which she sits ; like the vampire, she has been dead many times, and learned the secrets of the grave ; and has been a diver in deep seas, and keeps their fallen day about her ; and trafficked for strange webs with Eastern merchants : and, as Leda, was the mother of Helen of Troy, and, as Saint Anne, the mother of Mary ; and all this has been to her but as the sound of lyres and flutes, and lives only in the delicacy with which it has moulded the changing lineaments, and tinged the eyelids and the hands."

Such writing as this has an undeniable magic about it ; though its vagueness is not wholly characteristic of Pater's ordinary manner, it is a wonderful achievement ; it is more like a musical fantasia, embodying hints and echoes, touching with life a store of reveries and dreams, opening up strange avenues of dreamful thought, than a precise description of any actual work of art. To say that Leonardo himself would have disclaimed this interpretation of his picture is not to dispel the beauty of the criticism ; for the

magical power of art is its quickening spirit, its faculty
of touching trains of thought that run far beyond the
visible and bounding horizon. It is possible, too, to dislike the passage for its strong and luscious fragrance,
its overpowering sensuousness, to say that it is touched
with decadence, in its dwelling on the beauty of evil,
made fair by remoteness; but this is to take an ethical
view of it, to foresee contingencies, to apprehend the
ultimate force of its appeal. As in all lofty art, the
beauty is inexplicable, the charm incommunicable; its
sincerity, its zest is apparent; and it can hardly be
excelled as a typical instance of the prose that is
essentially poetical, in its liquid cadences, its echoing
rhythms. In any case, whether one feels the charm
of the passage or not, it must remain as perhaps the
best instance of Pater's early mastery of his art, in its
most elaborate and finished form.

The essay on the "School of Giorgione" is a later
work (1877), but it will be well to consider it here. It
is an elaborate composition, and shows a tendency to
return to metaphysical speculation, or rather to inter-
fuse a metaphysical tinge into artistic perception. He
lays down the principle that the quality of the particular medium of a work of art is what it is necessary
to discern, and that it is a mistake to blend the appeal
of different methods of artistic expression. "All art,"
he says in an italicised sentence, showing that he is
laying it down as an established maxim, "*constantly
aspires towards the condition of music,*" because music is
the only art which makes its appeal through pure form,
while all other art tends to have the motive confused by the matter, by the subject which it aims at
reproducing. "Music, then, and not poetry, as is so
often supposed," he adds, "is the true type or measure
of perfected art."

The attitude of Giorgione, his distinctive quality, lies, according to Pater, in the fact that " he is the inventor of *genre*, of those easily movable pictures which serve neither for uses of devotion, nor of allegorical or historic teaching—little groups of real men and women, amid congruous furniture or landscape—morsels of actual life, conversation or music or play, refined upon or idealised, till they come to seem like glimpses of life from afar." But one of the chief points of interest in the essay is that Pater devotes more space to his perception of music than he does in any other place. Giorgione himself was, according to traditions, an admirable musician, and musical scenes are made the motive of many of his pictures, or of those attributed to him : " music heard at the pool-side while people fish, or mingled with the sound of the pitcher in the well, or heard across running water, or among the flocks ; the tuning of instruments—people with intent faces, as if listening, like those described by Plato in an ingenious passage, to detect the smallest interval of musical sound, the smallest undulation in the air, or feeling for music in thought on a stringless instrument, ear and finger refining themselves infinitely, in the appetite for sweet sound—a momentary touch of an instrument in the twilight, as one passes through some unfamiliar room, in a chance company."

But the essay is not perhaps quite as lucid as some of the earlier work ; the tendency to construct long involved sentences, full of parentheses, is here apparent ; it gives one the impression of a vague musical modulation, which, beautiful in its changes, its relations, lacks the crispness and certainty of precise form.

There remains the " Joachim du Bellay," a slight essay where Pater occupies himself with showing how

Ronsard endeavoured to draw the influence of the Italian renaissance in to enliven and deepen the native Gothic material of French song, "gilding its surface with a strange delightful foreign aspect, like a chance effect of light." He indicates how, in that transformation, the old French seriousness disappeared, leaving nothing but "the elegance, the aërial touch, the perfect manner" in the poets of Ronsard's school, of whom Du Bellay was the last. Du Bellay strove with all his might, as in the little tract, *La Deffense et Illustration de la Langue Françoyse*," "to adjust the existing French culture to the rediscovered classical culture," "to ennoble the French language, to give it grace, number, perfection." Pater traces the eagerness for word-music, the beginnings of *poésie intime*, the poetry in which a writer strives to shape his innermost moods or to take the world into his confidence. He illustrates Du Bellay's fondness for landscape : "a sudden light transfigures a trivial thing, a weather-vane, a windmill, a winnowing flail, the dust in the barn door : a moment —and the thing has vanished, because it was pure effect ; but it leaves a relish behind it, a longing that the accident may happen again."

The whole essay is in a lighter, a less serious tone, and dwells more softly upon the surface of things ; and thus gives a kind of relief, a breathing space in the intense mood. One feels that some art went to the careful placing of these essays ; for we pass to the study on "Winckelmann," of which we have spoken at length, in which Pater found a type by which he might reveal his own inner thought, the conversion which he had experienced. And thus we come to the "Conclusion," a most elaborate texture of writing, made obscure by its compression, by its effort to catch and render the most complicated effects of thought. This "Conclusion" was omitted in the second edition of the book. Pater says that he excluded it, "as I conceived it might possibly mislead some of those young men into whose hands it might fall." He adds that he made a few changes which brought it closer to his original meaning, and that he had dealt more fully with the subject in *Marius the Epicurean.*

The only substantial alterations in the essay are as follows. Pater originally wrote :—

"High passions give one this quickened sense of life, ecstasy and sorrow of love, political or religious enthusiasm, or the 'enthusiasm of humanity.'"

This sentence became :—

"Great passions may give us this quickened sense of life, ecstasy and sorrow of love, the various forms of enthusiastic activity, disinterested or otherwise, which come naturally to many of us."

Again, in a passage dealing with the various ways of using life, so as to fill it full of beautiful energy, he says that "the wisest" spend it "in art and song." In the later version he qualifies the words "the wisest" by the addition of the phrase "at least among 'the children of this world.'"

The alterations do not appear at first sight to have any very great significance ; but Pater says that they brought out his original meaning more clearly ; and the very minuteness of the changes serves at least to show his sense of the momentousness of phrases.

He traces, in a passage of rich and subtle complexity, the bewildering effect upon the mind of the flood of external impressions ; and compares it with the thought that gradually emerges, as the spirit deals with these impressions, of the loneliness, the solitude of personality ; and with the mystery of the movement of time, the flight of the actual moment which is gone even while we try to apprehend it. He compares the perception to "a tremulous wisp constantly re-forming itself on the stream" of sense; and goes on to indicate that the aim of the perceptive mind should be to make the most of these fleeting moments, to "be present always at the focus where the greatest number of vital forces unite in their purest energy." "To burn always with this hard, gemlike flame, to maintain this ecstasy, is success in life." "Not to discriminate every moment some passionate attitude in those about us, is, on this short day of frost and sun, to sleep before evening."

He goes on to say that to get as many pulsations into the brief interval of life, is the one chance which is open to a man; and art, he says, gives most of these, "for art comes to you professing frankly to give nothing but the highest quality to your moments as they pass, and simply for those moments' sake."

The "Conclusion," then, is a presentment of the purest and highest Epicureanism, the Epicureanism that is a kind of creed, and realises the duty and necessity of activity and energy, but in a world of thought rather than of action. The peril of such a creed, of which Pater became aware, is that it is in the first place purely self-regarding, and in the second place that, stated in the form of abstract principles, it affords no bulwark against the temptation to sink from a pure and passionate beauty of perception into a grosser indulgence in sensuous delights. The difficulty in the artistic, as in the ethical scale, is to discern at what point the spirit begins to yield to the lower impulse; when it deserts the asceticism, the purity, the stainlessness of nature which alone can communicate that lucidity of vision, that seriousness of purpose, that

ordered simplicity of life that is to be the characteristic of the nobler Epicureanism.

Not that Pater withdrew the "Conclusion" because
he mistrusted his own principles ; such principles as he
held would tend to the refinement and enlargement of
the moral nature, by multiplying relationships, by
substituting sympathy for conscience, by admitting to
the full the loftier religious influences; and thus the
self-absorption of the artist would insensibly give place
to a wider, more altruistic absorption.

But Pater felt, no doubt, that having struck a sensuous note in his essays, this statement of principles of
artistic axioms lent itself to misrepresentation ; and
nothing could more clearly prove the affectionate considerateness of his nature, his desire for sympathy and
relationship, his tender care for those whom he loved
in spirit, than his fear of giving a wrong bias to their
outlook.   And thus the omission has a biographical
interest, as showing the first shadow of disapproval
falling on the sensitive mind, that disapproval which
sometimes hung like a cloud over Pater's enjoyment of
the world, though it never for a moment diverted him
from his serious and sustained purpose, as a prophet
of mysteries.

Pater's art criticism was distinctly of a literary and
traditional type.   He made little attempt to trace or
weigh the extrinsic value of works of art, or to discuss
the subject from the archæological or the technical
point of view.   He accepted the traditional knowledge
of the period, made no artistic discoveries, settled no
controverted points.   His concern was entirely with
the artistic merits of a picture and its poetical
suggestiveness ; his criticism, indeed, was of the type
which he defined in a review which he wrote many
years afterwards for the *Guardian* as "imaginative

criticism"—"that criticism which is itself a kind of construction, or creation, as it penetrates, through the given literary or artistic product, into the mental and inner constitution of the producer, shaping his work;" and thus the errors which he made, of which we may quote one or two examples, do not really affect the value of his criticism very greatly.

To take his criticism of Leonardo. He was certainly wrong, for instance, in his judgment of the Medusa picture. This is a picture which shows strong traces both of classical and realistic influences. The head is classical, the serpents are realistic. It is almost certainly at least a century later than Leonardo's period.

Again, the little head with the aureole of hair, which Pater had engraved for a frontispiece to the *Renaissance* as a genuine work of Leonardo's, is simply a school drawing, done under the influence, perhaps under the supervision, of Leonardo, by a pupil, but certainly not the work of the master's hand.

He makes, too, the general mistake of treating Leonardo as a realist. But there is no basis of truth in this. The influence of realism had not begun to be felt at his date, or at all events in his work. The studies, for instance, to which Pater alludes, as of various flowers, of which there are a number of instances in the Windsor collection, are not realistically treated, but conventionally, and with the influence of tradition strongly marked in them.

Again it will be remembered how Pater speaks of the angel's head, which according to tradition Leonardo contributed to a picture of his master, Verrocchio. He says that the head is still to be seen, "a space of sunlight in the cold, laboured, old picture." There are in reality two heads in the picture, probably both by

D

Leonardo, and one curiously ill-drawn. But the picture is not cold and laboured; it is simply unfinished, and not in a condition on which a judgment of its possibilities could be passed.

In the essay on "Botticelli" he was on firmer ground. But the essay on the "School of Giorgione" is perhaps the most typical instance. There are only two Giorgiones which can be positively identified as his from contemporary records. These are the picture known as "The Three Philosophers," or "The Chaldean Sages," which is now supposed by some critics to represent the arrival of Æneas in Italy; and the picture known as "The Stormy Landscape" in the Giovanelli Palace at Venice, which is now sometimes called "Adrastus and Hypsipyle." Then there is the great Castelfranco altar-piece, which by tradition and internal evidence may be held to be an indubitable Giorgione. Then there are others with a reasonable degree of probability, such as the "Knight in Armour" in the National Gallery, said to be a study for the figure of S. Liberale in the Castelfranco altar-piece, an "Adoration of the Shepherds," belonging to Mr. Wentworth Beaumont, and two panels at Florence, one representing an incident in the legendary childhood of Moses, and the other "The Judgment of Solomon." But "The Concert," in the Pitti, cannot be certainly attributed to Giorgione, and it may be said that the more Pater had known about Giorgione, the less likely would he have been to have attributed the picture to him. The truth is that Giorgione is a somewhat legendary painter, and what work of his is authentic is probably his later work. Art critics have of course as far as possible to account for the existence of such a legend; but the result is that in Pater's hands, with the faulty and imperfect knowledge that

existed about Giorgione at the time when he wrote,
the subject is misconceived and exaggerated. There
is, in the authentic works of Giorgione, an almost entire
want of dramatic unity. In "The Stormy Landscape,"
for instance, the figures of the mother with an infant
and the young knight have no connection with each
other, and are both entirely out of keeping with and
unaffected by the scene, where the storm is breaking
in thunder and rain. So, too, in "The Judgment of
Solomon" panel there is no concentration of motive ;
each figure is conceived separately, and there is no
sort of attempt at dramatic combination.

But when all this has been said, it really affects very
little the value of Pater's work. After all, the pictures
which he described exist; the message which they held
for his own spirit was generated by the sight of them,
and the poetical suggestiveness of his criticism is full
of vital force ; he made no attempt to set misconception right, to date pictures, or to alter their dates. He
took them on trust ; and thus, though his judgments
have no precise technical value, the inspiration of his
sympathetic emotion forfeits little or none of its force
by being expended on pictures which he did not attribute correctly, and which it could not be expected that
he should have so attributed.

The publication of the *Renaissance* was to be attended
by important results. It gave Pater a definite place in
the literary and artistic world. But it had a still
deeper effect. The spirit of artistic revolt was in the
air. The writings of Ruskin, the work of the Pre-
Raphaelites may be taken as two salient instances in
very different regions of the rising tendency. What
underlay the whole movement was a desire to treat art
seriously, and to give it its place in the economy of
human influences. Side by side with this was a strong

vein of discontent with established theories of religion, of education, of mental cultivation. The younger generation was thrilled with a sense of high artistic possibilities; it realised that there was a hidden treasure of accumulated art, ancient and medieval, which remained as a living monument of certain brilliant and glowing forces that seemed to have become quiescent. It became aware that it was existing under cramped conditions, in a comfortable barbarism, encompassed by strict and respectable traditions, living a bourgeois kind of life, fettered by a certain stupid grossness, a life that checked the free development of the soul.

Pater's suggestive and poetical treatment of medieval art fired a train, and tended to liberate an explosive revolutionary force of artistic feeling which manifested itself in intemperate extravagances for which he was indeed in no sense responsible, but which could be to a certain extent referred to his principles. Young men with vehement impulses, with no experience of the world, no idea of the solid and impenetrable weight of social traditions and prejudices, found in the principles enunciated by Pater with so much recondite beauty, so much magical charm, a new equation of values. Pater himself was to pay dearly for his guileless sincerity, his frank confidence.

In 1877, the year in which the second edition of the *Renaissance* was issued, appeared Mr. Mallock's *New Republic*. It is a difficult question to decide to what extent a satire of the kind is justifiable. It was an extraordinarily suggestive and humorous book; and the author would no doubt justly maintain that in Mr. Rose he was merely parodying a type of the aesthetic school; but language was put into Mr. Rose's mouth which was obviously a faithful parody of Pater's style

of writing, with an added touch of languor and extravagance. The bitterness of the satire was increased by
its being cast in a conversational form, so that it would
be concluded by those who did not know Pater that
his conversation in a mixed society was couched in this
exotic and affected vein, reaching a degree of grotesque-
ness on the one hand and sensuousness on the other
which was bound to produce an unpleasant effect on
the minds of readers. Mr. Rose is made to discourse
in public in a dreamy vein in a manner which draws
from Lady Ambrose, a conventional and worldly person,
the comment that he always speaks of every one "as if
they had no clothes on." But there are more disagree-
able innuendoes than that; and as it was inevitable
from the language employed that Mr. Rose should be
identified with Pater, it is hard to absolve the author
from the charge of sacrificing the scrupulous justice
that should have been shown to an individual to the
desire for effectiveness and humour, though on the
other hand an ample excuse is afforded in the youthful
ebullience of the book, written, it is marvellous to reflect, when the author was still an undergraduate.
Pater had indeed laid himself in one sense open to the
attack, by committing to the impersonal medium of a
book sentiments which could be distorted into the
sensuous creed of aesthetes; to satirise the advanced
type of the aesthetic school was perfectly fair, but it was
unduly harsh to cause an affected and almost licentious
extravagance of behaviour to be attributed to one
whose private life and conversation were of so sober
and simple a character. It seems clear that the satire
caused Pater considerable distress. If he had been
personally vain or socially ambitious, it might have
gratified him to be included in so distinguished a company; but all this was entirely foreign to his retired

and studious habits; he did not at all desire to have a
mysterious and somewhat painful prestige thrust upon
him; and though he seldom if ever spoke of the subject
even to his most intimate friends, yet it is impossible
not to realise that the satire must have caused him
sincere pain. It was in this mood that he said to Mr.
Gosse, "I wish they wouldn't call me a 'hedonist'; it
produces such a bad effect on the minds of people
who don't know Greek." He felt that he had been
deliberately misrepresented, made unjustly notorious,
and the sober and strenuous ideal of his life cruelly
obscured.

Although Pater had been a pupil of Jowett's, and
although there was a *rapprochement* in later life, when
Jowett took occasion warmly to congratulate Pater on
his *Plato and Platonism*, there was a misunderstanding
of some kind which resulted in a dissidence between
them in the middle years. It has even been said that
Jowett took up a line of definite opposition to Pater,
and used his influence to prevent his obtaining University work and appointments. It is not impossible
that this was the case. Jowett, in spite of his genius,
in spite of his liberality of view and his deliberate
tolerance, was undoubtedly an opportunist. He was
not exactly guided by the trend of public opinion, but
he took care not to back men or measures unless he
would be likely to have the support of a strong section
of the community, or at least conceived it probable that
his line would eventually be endorsed by public opinion.
Thus his religious position was based not on the fact
that he wished to be in opposition to popular ortho-
doxy, but that he followed an enlightened line, with
a belief that, in the long-run, the best intelligence of
the country would adopt similar views. That this is
not an over-statement is clear from Jowett's *Life*, where

he is revealed as a far more liberal, even destructive critic of popular religion than he allowed to appear in either his writings or public utterances.

Probably Jowett either identified Pater with the advanced aesthetic school, or supposed that at all events his teaching was adapted to strengthen a species of Hedonism, or modern Paganism, which was alien to the spirit of the age. Or possibly he was alarmed at the mental and moral attitude with which Pater was publicly credited, owing in considerable measure to the appearance of the *New Republic*—in which he himself was pilloried as the representative of advanced religious liberalism—and thought that on public grounds he must combat the accredited leaders of a movement which was certainly unfashionable, and which was regarded with suspicion by men of practical minds. Whatever his motives were, he certainly meant to make it plain that he did not desire to see the supposed exponents of the aesthetic philosophy holding office in the University.

One feels that Jowett, with his talent for frank remonstrance, had better have employed direct rather than indirect methods; but the fact remains that he not only disliked the tendency of Pater's thought, but endeavoured, by means that are invariably ineffectual, to subvert his influence.

It is not difficult to arrive at Pater's view of Jowett; he regarded his qualities, both administrative and mental, with a considerable degree of admiration. He half envied and was half amused by the skilful way in which Jowett contrived, taught by adversity and opposition, to harmonise advanced religious views with popular conceptions, and to subordinate philosophical speculation to practical effectiveness. He considered him an excellent specimen of the best kind of

virtuous sophist. A letter on the subject which he
contributed in 1894 to the *Life of Jowett* is interesting.

Speaking of his own undergraduate days, he says
that Jowett's generosity in the matter of giving undergraduates help and encouragement in their work was
unprecedented,

" on the part of one whose fame among the youth, though he
was then something of a recluse, was already established.
Such fame rested on his great originality as a writer and
thinker. He seemed to have taken the measure not merely
of all opinions, but of all possible ones, and to have put the
last refinements on literary expression. The charm of that
was enhanced by a certain mystery about his own philosophic
and other opinions. You know at that time his writings were
thought by some to be obscure. These impressions of him
had been derived from his Essays on St. Paul's Epistles,
which at that time were much read and pondered by the more
intellectual sort of undergraduates. When he lectured on
Plato, it was a fascinating thing to see those qualities as if in
the act of creation, his lectures being informal, unwritten, and
seemingly unpremeditated, but with many a long-remembered
gem of expression, or delightfully novel idea, which seemed to
be lying in wait whenever, at a loss for a moment in his somewhat hesitating discourse, he opened a book of loose notes.
They passed very soon into other note-books all over the University ; the larger part, but I think not all of them, into his
published introductions to the *Dialogues*. Ever since I heard
it, I have been longing to read a very dainty dialogue on
language, which formed one of his lectures, a sort of ' New
Cratylus.' "

At the same time Pater had no sort of inner sympathy with Jowett's position as a priest of the Anglican
Church, considering the opinions on the subject of
Christian doctrine which he held, or which Pater
believed him to hold. There is practically no doubt

that in the review of *Robert Elsmere* which Pater contributed to the *Guardian*, he had Jowett in his mind in
the following passage :—

"Of course, a man such as Robert Elsmere came to be
ought not to be a clergyman of the Anglican Church.   The
priest is still, and will, we think, remain, one of the necessary
types of humanity ; and he is untrue to his type, unless, with
whatever inevitable doubts in this doubting age, he feels, on
the whole, the preponderance in it of those influences which
make for faith.   It is his triumph to achieve as much faith as
possible in an age of negation.   Doubtless, it is part of the ideal
of the Anglican Church that, under certain safeguards, it
should find room for latitudinarians even among its clergy.
Still, with these, as with all other genuine priests, it is the
positive not the negative result that justifies the position.   We
have little patience with those liberal clergy who dwell on
nothing else than the difficulties of faith and the propriety of
concession to the opposite force."

The truth is that the two temperaments were radically opposed, though they had certain philosophical
interests in common.   At bottom Jowett was a man
of the world, and valued effectiveness above most
qualities ; while Pater set no particular value upon
administrative energy.   Jowett was indifferent to art,
except in so far as it ministered to agreeable social
intercourse ; with Pater art provided what were the
deepest and most sacred experiences of his life.   Not
until Pater became a growing power in the literary
and artistic world, not until it became clear that
he had no practical sympathy with the exponents
of a bastard aestheticism, did Jowett recognise the
fame of his former pupil ; and as the respect of Jowett,
when conceded to persons with whom he did not
agree, may be recognised as having a certain value of
barometrical indication, as reflecting the opinion of the

world in a species of enlightened mirror, we may consider that Jowett's expressed admiration of *Plato and Platonism* was a belated admission that Pater had indubitably attained to the eminence which the Professor of Greek had long before prophesied for him.

CHAPTER III

OXFORD LIFE

THE years that succeeded the first publication of the *Renaissance* were not years of very strenuous literary work. Pater was at this time holding the Tutorship of the College, as well as lecturing, and the official business connected with the post was considerable. A tutor is supposed to exert a general supervision over the work of his pupils, to criticise their compositions and essays, and to keep himself informed of their progress. It cannot be said that Pater's practical effectiveness was strong enough to equip him adequately for the task. He received and criticised the essays; he responded with cordial sympathy to any direct appeals for assistance; but a tutor, to be effective, must have a power of shining, like the sun, upon the eager and the reluctant, the grateful and the unthankful alike; some pupils must be impulsively inspired; some delicately encouraged; some ironically chastised; some few must, like the image of Democracy in Tennyson's poem, "toil onward, prick'd with goads and stings."

Pater had little capacity for this kind of work—indeed, he did not even conceive it to be his duty; but in any case the mere routine-work was heavy. Moreover, he had to a certain extent come out of his shell, enjoyed a good deal of quiet sociability, and gained a reputation as a brilliant and paradoxical talker.

Meanwhile, as I have said, his literary output was small. His study of "Wordsworth" (1874) is a very subtle piece of criticism. It is often taken for granted that Wordsworth valued tranquillity above ardour, and thus the essay is peculiarly felicitous in pointing out that not mere contemplation, but *impassioned* contemplation, was the underlying purpose of the poet's life. Pater shows that Wordsworth's choice of incidents and situations from common life was made "not for their tameness, but for (their) passionate sincerity." He indicates that the reason why Wordsworth selected the homelier figures of the world for his protagonists was that he might display "all the pathetic episodes of their humble existence, their longing, their wonder at fortune, their poor pathetic pleasures, like the pleasures of children, won so hardly in the struggle for bare existence ; their yearning towards each other, in their darkened houses, or at their early toil."

It is too customary with critics to draw a sharp line between Wordsworth in his moments of inspired passion and Wordsworth in the mood of solemn ineffectiveness; and thus those who write on Wordsworth too often view his work with a certain impatience, as if by an effort he could have criticised himself, and made a more emphatic selection of his own writings. But Pater, though he echoes the wish that Wordsworth could have been more severe in the matter of omission, shows the essential unity of his work, arising from the deliberate passivity with which he waited dutifully upon the gift of inspiration ; and he compares him beautifully to "one of those early Italian or Flemish painters, who, just because their minds were full of heavenly visions, passed, some of them, the better part of sixty years in quiet, systematic industry."

In fact, Pater realised, perhaps unconsciously, that what Wordsworth had written in the "Poet's Epitaph" was as true of Wordsworth himself;—"And you must love him, ere to you he will seem worthy of your love"; and thus the spirit in which he deals with Wordsworth's work is one of a reverent tenderness, that cannot even bear to speak with the least roughness or harshness of the writings of one so sincere, so wise, so deep-hearted, even when engaged in the task of producing arid and pompous couplets, or rubbing, as Matthew Arnold says, like Indians in primeval forests, one dry stick upon another in the hope of generating a flame.

Pater is particularly alive to Wordsworth's deep sense of what may be called the *admonitus locorum*, the local sanctities, the far-reaching human associations with places, dealing with them largely, "till the low walls, the green mounds, the half-obliterated epitaphs seemed full of voices."

Again, Pater skilfully divines Wordsworth's peculiar power "of realising, and conveying to the consciousness of the reader, abstract and elementary impressions —silence, darkness, absolute motionlessness : or, again, the whole complex sentiment of a particular place, the abstract expression of desolation in the long white road, of peacefulness in a particular folding of the hills."

It is abundantly clear that, in the case of Wordsworth, Pater felt himself drawing near to a highly congenial personality. He speaks in another essay of the poet's "flawless temperament, his fine mountain atmosphere of mind." The dignity, the seriousness, the quietness, the impassioned quality of the poet's life made a strong appeal to him, and not less the high purpose to which he dedicated his whole life: the rendering and interpreting of beautiful impressions, the desire to impart to others what gave him joy and tranquillity; and thus the whole essay is redolent of a sort of trustful affection, the mood in which a man speaks simply and sincerely of a point of view which he instinctively admires, a character that is very dear to his heart. Pater goes, indeed, so far as to say in a later essay that a careful reading of Wordsworth is probably the very best thing that can be found to counteract the faults and offences of our busy and restless generation, as helping to remind us, "amid the enormous expansion of all that is material and mechanical in life, of the essential value, the permanent ends, of life itself."

The essay on "Charles Lamb" (1878) is another instance of Pater's power of selecting and emphasising the congenial elements of a character. It is not the inconsequent, the reckless humour of Charles Lamb that Pater values most, his power of pursuing a humorous image, of clinging to it, as Lamb did among the rubs and adversities of the world, as a man in a beating sea might cling to a spar for his life. Pater is rather in love with the contrast of Lamb's life, the tragic undercurrent of fate, that ran like a dark stream below his lightness, his pathetic merriment. He admires him as an artist first, because "in the making of prose he realises the principle of art for its own sake, as completely as Keats in the making of verse." He values him for the "little arts of happiness he is ready to teach to others," for his deep and patient friendships; he sees in him "a lover of household warmth everywhere," a collector of things which gain a colour for him "by the little accidents which attest previous ownership." He loves him because he "has a care for the sighs, and the weary, humdrum preoccupations

of very weak people, down to their little pathetic
'gentilities,' even; while, in the purely human temper,
he can write of death, almost like Shakespeare."
"Unoccupied," he says, "as he might seem, with great
matters, he is in immediate contact with what is real,
especially in its caressing littleness, that littleness in
which there is much of the whole woeful heart of
things, and meets it more than half-way with a perfect
understanding of it." He realises, too, the fineness
and largeness of Lamb's criticism; he says that when
Lamb comments on Shakespeare, he is like "a man
who walks alone under a grand stormy sky, and among
unwonted tricks of light, when powerful spirits might
seem to be abroad upon the air"; and he does, too,
full justice to Lamb's poetical appreciation of London.
"Nowhere," he says, in the melodious concluding sentence, "is there so much difference (as in London)
between rain and sunshine, nowhere do the clouds
roll together more grandly . . . the background of
the great city, with its weighty atmosphere, and por-
tent of storm in the rapid light on dome and bleached
stone steeples."

Perhaps it may be thought that Pater's judgment
of Lamb is coloured by too strong an infusion of his
own personality, and that the Charles Lamb of the
essay is hardly recognisable, clothed, as he appears to
be, in his critic's very wardrobe; that Pater puts aside
certain broad aspects of Lamb's character as being less
congenial to himself; but I should rather myself feel
that he has indeed passed behind the smiling mask
which Lamb often wore, or has, perhaps, persuaded
him to doff it; and that he has thus got nearer, in
fact, to this melancholy loving spirit, with its self-
condemned indulgences, its vein of mockery, its long
spaces of dreariness, its acute sensibilities. Lamb,

one feels, was a pilgrim in hard places, and, like
Bunyan's pilgrims, caught desperately at the fruits
that hung over the wall, to relieve his sadness; and
yet, in another mood, he was full of a tender quietism,
with a large and loving outlook upon humanity and
life. Pater seems to have come from reading Lamb
like a friend who has been communing with a friend.
They have talked without affectation and without dis-
guises; and thus one feels that, though there has been,
under the influence of sympathy, a certain suppression
or suspension of modes of speech, of aspects of thought,
that had a real bearing on Lamb's character, yet that
Pater has seen the innermost heart of the man with
the insight that only affection can give, an insight
which subtler and harder critics seem to miss, even
though the picture they may draw is incontestably
truer to detail.

Besides these two critical appreciations, Pater wrote
at this time a Shakespearian study, and the little essay
on "Romanticism," which re-appeared in 1889 as the
Postscript to *Appreciations*, which may be shortly discussed here.

It has a high value. It is a careful attempt to find a
definition for the two terms *classical* and *romantic*. Pater
sees with perspicuous clearness that one of the difficulties of finding a precise formula for large terms,
expressive of tendency, is the disentangling them
from the loose, conventional, and conversational sense
that they come to bear. Thus he says of the word
classical, that "it has often been used in a hard, and
merely scholastic sense, by the praisers of what is old and
accustomed, at the expense of what is new, by critics
who would never have discovered for themselves the
charm of any work, whether new or old, who value
what is old, in art or literature, for its accessories, and

chiefly for the conventional authority that has gathered about it—people who would never really have been made glad by any Venus fresh-risen from the sea, and who praise the Venus of old Greece and Rome, only because they fancy her grown now into something staid and tame."

He says that the charm of classical literature is the charm of the "well-known tale, to which we can, nevertheless, listen over and over again, because it is told so well. To the absolute beauty of its artistic form, is added the accidental, tranquil, charm of familiarity." "It comes to us out of the cool and quiet of other times, as the measure of what a long experience has shown will at least never displease us."

But the romantic spirit is that which craves for new motives, new subjects of interest, new modifications of style : its essence is the addition of strangeness to beauty ; its danger is to value what is after all inartistic—anything that is bizarre, strained, exaggerated. Pater contrasts Pope and Balzac as instances of the defects of the two styles,—Pope's lack of curiosity producing insipidity, and Balzac's excess of curiosity not being duly tempered with the desire of beauty ; and with singular felicity he selects the *Philoctetes* of Sophocles as a typically romantic book, but yet with all the tranquillity of the classical spirit.

Pater shows that romanticism generally arises, as in France with Rousseau, after a long period of stagnation and ennui. But after all, the essence of the situation lies in the fact that, as Stendhal says, all good art was romantic in its day ; and thus the charm of romanticism is the charm of the spring, of the unfolding of new forms, and strangely shaped flowers, and scented fruits ; the charm of classicism is the charm that creeps over the same landscape with the mellow

E

richness of autumn; and Pater sums up the whole subject by saying that "in truth, the legitimate contention is, not of one age or school of literary art against another, but of all successive schools alike, against the stupidity which is dead to the substance, and the vulgarity which is dead to form."

The conclusion, then, for Pater, is that our work should unite the true qualities of both romanticism and classicalism; that it should be fresh, new, spontaneous, and unconventional; decorous, but not hampered by decorum; gaining soberness and richness from recognised methods and due authority; but in the truest sense a development, neither a new departure nor a servile imitation. We are not to think slightingly of the old forms, or to neglect the hallowed influences of association; authority must control the manner, vitality suggest the matter. And in all this Pater is true to his creed, clinging as he did to the old forms of melodies and enriching them with new harmonies. He is content, indeed, to look backwards with reverent eyes upon the past; but he is all alive with the problems of the present, the hopes of the future.

And thus the essay comes to have a direct value, because in it he summarises and reflects, stating the truth positively, and not by allusion and in allegories. It is in a sense one of the manifestoes scattered through his writings; and it testifies to his belief, which one might forget in his dwelling upon the old and the established, that he was in heart upon the side of the new, the inquisitive, the expansive; that his work indeed is only critical in form, but essentially creative in spirit.

He wrote too, at this time, the essay on the "School of Giorgione," which was added to the *Renaissance* essays in the third edition, and which has already been discussed. But his main concern was with the *Greek Studies*. "Demeter and Persephone" was delivered in the form of two lectures at the Birmingham and Midland Institute in 1875 and appeared in the *Fortnightly Review* in 1876. In the same year and in the same magazine appeared the "Dionysus." As, then, the most solid and vigorous sections of the *Greek Studies* were the work of these years, it will be better to speak of the book here, rather than at the date of its eventual publication (1895).

I do not mean here to dwell at any great length upon the volume, beautiful as the *Studies* are, because they are so strongly intermingled with the antiquarian and the scholarly element that they require a familiarity with classical learning, a special sort of initiation, to comprehend them. They are fully but not heavily freighted with erudition, and testify to a long and patient accumulation of facts and traditions. When the accumulation was complete—and it must have been a task of great labour—the details had to be touched as lightly and placed as expressively as possible. And they thus stand as an excellent work of art, and testify to the shaping into finished and balanced studies of a mass of technical and professional material.

To indicate them briefly in detail, the first is a study of "Dionysus," which touches with innumerable mystical and poetical suggestions the bright, gay, ruthless figure of the god, alive from head to foot, thrilling with the joy of life and beauty, and, with a divinely unassailed temperance of his own ; as he passes lightly in his robe of skins, poising his wand with the bare brown arm, carrying in his hand the strange secret of the vine, its heady visions, its power of overwhelming by a sort of resistless, poisonous energy the mortal spirit, heightening and gilding on the one hand its bright

fancies and sparkling dreams into a sort of mysterious
rapture, an inner careless glee ; and on the other hand
sinking melancholy thoughts into an abandoned and
exaggerated grief, and at last merging both joy and
grief together into a deep stupor of mind and body.
We Northerners, with the inherited taste for potent
and ardent beverages, as resources to fight against our
cheerless skies, our damp mists, our aching frosts, enlightened, too, by the later researches of natural philosophers, who have explained the magic of intoxication
as a sort of unseemly poisoning of mind and body
alike, are apt to view the effects of wine as an essentially grotesque and commonplace thing; we forget
what a mystery this fierce excitement, this strange im-
ported ecstasy of soul, the cloudy following lethargy
might mean, would mean to those to whom the whole
of life was a commerce with the divine, and who felt
themselves surrounded by secret and unseen influences.
And then, too, we must bear in mind that tendency of
personification which lay so close to the heart of these
old nations.   With us it is all the other way ; we tend
to refer all things to a vast unity of law, to prodigious
impersonal forces, thereby drawing, no doubt, nearer to
truth, but further and further away from the romance
that appeals to simple minds.

Thus to the Greeks the worship of the grape was
a discerning of "the spirit of fire and dew, alive and
leaping in a thousand vines."   The rites of Dionysus
were holy things, "breaths of remote nature . . . the
pines, the foldings of the hills, the leaping streams, the
strange echoings and dying of sound on the heights."
Dionysus, thus, was a spirit of fire and dew ; of fire
first :—

"And who," says Pater, "that has rested a hand on the
glittering silex of a vineyard slope in August, where the pale

globes of sweetness are lying, does not feel this ? It is out of the bitter salts of a smitten, volcanic soil that it comes up with the most curious virtues. . . . In thinking of Dionysus, then, as fire-born, the Greeks apprehend and embody the sentiment, the poetry, of all tender things which grow out of a hard soil, or in any sense blossom before the leaf, like the little mezereon-plant of English gardens, with its pale-purple, wine-scented flowers upon the leafless twigs in February, or like the almond-trees of Tuscany, or Aaron's rod that budded, or the staff in the hand of the Pope when Tannhäuser's repentance is accepted."

And then, too, Dionysus is born of the dew—of the freshness, the solace of liquid in a hot land.

"Think of the darkness of the well in the breathless court, with the delicate ring of ferns kept alive just within the opening ; of the sound of the fresh water flowing through the wooden pipes into the houses of Venice, on summer mornings."

It is this combining of symbolism that Pater believes to be so characteristic of the Greek sentiment: "the religious imagination of the Greeks being, precisely, a unifying or identifying power, bringing together things naturally asunder, making, as it were, for the human body a soul of waters, for the human soul a body of flowers."

And with it all, in the conception of this mystical impassioned Deity, goes a deep sadness, the sadness of one who is old though everlastingly young, who has seen a thousand fair things fade, year after year, the flowers withering in the sheltered places, the trees losing their rich summer foliage ; he has seen generation after generation arise in grace and beauty, thirsting for life, coming with new wonder to taste the sweet mysteries ; and they too have gone ; he knows the secrets of the grave ; he knows that though new life arises, the old life, the old passionate identities are not

restored.   He himself defies death and the violence
of traitorous people, infuriated by the sorrows that
follow so hard in the path of joy; he is slain, but
arises again with strength renewed and sadness increased; thus the vision glows, and fades, and glows
again.

It is in vain to ask ourselves whether the whole of
this body of symbolism was ever present in any mind
or group of minds.   That is not the concern of Pater;
his thought is rather to trace the many clear streams
that have ever flowed within the single channel.   He
gathers the waters in a heap, as the prophet of old said.
And the value of the essay is that it reveals something
of the freshness and richness of the Greek mind, the
exquisite power of seeing the beauty of sweet and
simple things, of interweaving them into joyful fancies,
embodying them into strange high-hearted tales; this
tendency is the exact opposite of our own Celtic
tendency, which loses itself in a vague and wistful
melancholy in the thought of desolate spirits full of
sorrow, that find their natural home in the soft weeping
world, the moors in which the rain drops pitifully, the
lonely hills.   With the Greeks the sense of presences
behind life, hovering near, revealing themselves in half-
glimpses, took shape in the bright sparkling pageant of
life—life that is determined in its brief space to press
out the most poignant qualities of sorrow and laughter,
of love and song.

In the "Bacchanals of Euripides" the same point is
touched on a different side; here we see the intoxicat-
ing sense of life and spring, the tingling impulse of the
dance, coming out in the group of worshippers, the
women who surround the woman-like god, touching
thought exclusively through the senses.   To these was
given to feel "the presence of night, the expectation of

morning, the nearness of wild, unsophisticated, natural things—the echoes, the coolness, the noise of frightened creatures as they climbed through the darkness, the sunrise seen from the hill-tops, the disillusion, the bitterness of satiety, the deep slumber which comes with the morning."

Pater traces the plot of the strange beauty-haunted play, with its grotesque episodes, such as the indignity of the Bacchic passion seizing upon the old fatuous men, horribly renewing their youth in a kind of shameless parody of childish merriment, up to the appalling tragedy of the end, the doom of scepticism that yet involves a house and a nation in speechless grief and horror.

In "The Myth of Demeter and Persephone," which Pater said had been the most laborious and difficult piece of work he had ever done, he traces the complex shadowy legend from its early origins. The Mother of Nature, with her power over the kindly fruits of the earth, is first depicted ; and then in the midst of her passionless content, her easy benevolence, her daughter is snatched away to be queen among the dead ; the mother, in a sad indifference of grief, sets out stony-hearted on the quest, sometimes blasting, sometimes blessing the earth through which she passes, losing, in the stress of that bitter sorrow, the balance of mind, the responsibility, which her influence had brought her. Pater shows that behind all the brightness, the hopefulness, the impassioned geniality of the Greek creed, there lay a shadow.—

"The 'worship of sorrow,' as Goethe called it, is sometimes supposed to have had almost no place in the religion of the Greeks. Their religion has been represented as a religion of mere cheerfulness, the worship by an untroubled, unreflecting humanity, conscious of no deeper needs, of the embodi-

ments of its own joyous activity. It helped to hide out of
their sight those traces of decay and weariness, of which the
Greeks were constitutionally shy, to keep them from peeping
too curiously into certain shadowy places, appropriate enough
to the gloomy imagination of the middle age ; and it hardly
proposed to itself to give consolation to people who, in truth,
were never ' sick or sorry.' But this familiar view of Greek
religion is based on a consideration of a part only of what is
known concerning it, and really involves a misconception, akin
to that which underestimates the influence of the romantic
spirit generally, in Greek poetry and art ; as if Greek art had
dealt exclusively with human nature in its sanity, suppressing
all motives of strangeness, all the beauty which is born of
difficulty, permitting nothing but an Olympian, though perhaps somewhat wearisome calm. In effect, such a conception
of Greek art and poetry leaves in the central expressions of
Greek culture none but negative qualities ; and the legend of
Demeter and Persephone, perhaps the most popular of all
Greek legends, is sufficient to show that the ' worship of
sorrow' was not without its function in Greek religion ; their
legend is a legend made by and for sorrowful, wistful, anxious
people ; while the most important artistic monuments of that
legend sufficiently prove that the Romantic spirit was really
at work in the minds of Greek artists, extracting by a kind of
subtle alchemy, a beauty, not without the elements of tranquillity, of dignity and order, out of a matter, at first sight
painful and strange."

But perhaps the most important dictum which Pater
lays down in the essay is this—that "in the applica-
tion of these theories, the student of Greek religion
must never forget that, after all, it is with poetry, not
with systematic theological belief or dogma, that he has
to do."

In the second part of the essay he traces the
myth through its treatment by many hands, the hands
of poets, the hands of sculptors, each adding something
of their own restless and eager personality to these

figures of the "goddesses of the earth, akin to the influence of cool places, quiet houses, subdued light, tranquillising voices."

It is here that he conceives the secret to lie—that in the perceptions of these old imaginings we may not only draw nearer to the heart of the ancient world, but that they may bring us too, by sweet association and delicate shadowy imagery, some uplifting and enlarging of our own sympathies and hopes.

The "Hippolytus Veiled" (1889) is a much later work, but it will be as well to treat of it here, though it belongs less to the stricter archæological studies, and more to the series of *Imaginary Portraits*. Pater takes the old sad legend of Hippolytus, the child of Theseus and an Amazon, the type of a stainless and almost froward chastity, which brings with it the penalty of the scorning of divine influence, of natural law ; and embroiders out of it an elaborate and beautiful story, heaped with rich and fervid accessories. He points out first the exquisite finish, the clear-cut detail, which characterises even the smallest and daintiest of Greek legends ; " the impression of Greece generally," he says, "is but enhanced by the littleness of the physical scene of events intellectually so great—such a system of grand lines, restrained within so narrow a compass, as in one of its fine coins." And thus he illustrates that salient characteristic of Greek life—the absence of centralisation, the intensity with which so vivid a life burnt sharply at so many provincial centres simultaneously. Then comes the story, the noble child so carefully nurtured by the desolate sorrowing mother, acquiring in and through her woe all the arts of simple seemly living, in order that she may delicately nurture the child of her fall. Pater brings the lonely cave-life before one—the wax-tapers, the hunger of the boy so daintily satisfied, his eager prattling alertness, the joyful days, overshadowed only by the thought that they were surely passing. Then the boy passes on to the greater world, becomes renowned in all manly exercises, but keeps his purity unsullied, even in the perfumed chambers of the palace, face to face with the feverish desire of the shameless Phædra. "He had a marvellous air of discretion about him, as of one never to be caught unaware, as if he never could be anything but like water from the rock, or the wild flowers of the morning, or the beams of the morning star turned to human flesh." Repulsed and mad with jealous shame, Phædra whispers the traitorous tale to Theseus, who utters a curse upon the boy, so that he falls into a wasting sickness. Even so the gods are merciful; he struggles back to life, to lose it again before the wrath of Poseidon, or even perhaps of Aphrodite herself, as he drives his chariot along the shore. The earth rocks, a great wave whitens on the beach; the horses plunge and start, and he is buffeted to death among the sea-boulders and the crawling brine.

The tale has a curious magic about it; but though Greek in outline, it is hardly Greek in quality, suffused as it is with a strange and wistful romance that is born of a later and more self-conscious age.

In the essays on the "Beginnings of Greek Sculpture" he touches on the possibilities of external influences, the hints from the East, from Egypt, Assyria, Phœnicia, Asia Minor, Cyprus, as forming possibly the seed of Greek art. But he points out truly that this art is all "emphatically *autochthonous*, as the Greeks said, new-born at home, by right of a new, informing, combining spirit playing over those mere elements, and touching them, above all, with a wonderful sense of the nature and destiny of man—the dignity of his soul and of his body—so that in all things the Greeks are as discoverers."

And he points out, too, that we are apt to import too purely an intellectual element into our conceptions of Greek art, because we have to deal with it principally in the form of sculpture, the only product that remains to us in large measure, while their pictures, their metal work, their carvings, their embroideries, have suffered a natural decay. Pater deals first with the descriptions of ancient shields, and with the excavated treasures of Mycenæ, and points out that this metal-work, with its special *cachet*, "the seal of nearness to the workman's hand," and the Greek tendency to overlay stone as far as possible with metal, show that Greek art probably first displayed itself in this form, and was in reality the expression of an age of gold rather than of stone.

In the second essay he traces the growth of true sculpture, the gradual preference of marble as a medium for art, until the first school of sculptors appears at Sicyon, the chief seat in earliest days of Greek art. Here he depends mostly upon the authority of Pausanias ; "our own fancy," he says, "must fill up the story of the unrecorded patience of the workshop, into which we seem to peep through these scanty notices— the fatigue, the disappointments, the steps repeated, ending at last in that moment of success, which is all Pausanias records, somewhat uncertainly."

He shows that in the detachment of images from the walls and pillars behind them, Greek art was already liberated from its earlier Eastern associations, which worked only in reliefs and friezes ; and then came the perception that sculpture was not to be a thing of mechanical and mathematical proportions, but the representation of a living organism with free-

dom of movement, full of the human soul, instead of a
mere stiff attitude and a frozen gesture.

And then religion comes in to swell the richness
of art, and the vague customs and traditions of the
older days transform themselves into the breathing
images of personal gods enshrined and enthroned.

The essay ends with an attempt to indicate the
characteristics of the great school of Sicyon as represented by Canachus—a sculptor, it would seem, of deep
religious feeling, and distinguished by that early stiff
naïveté of work which indicates " a gravity, a discretion
and reserve, the charm of which, if felt in quiet, is
hardly less than that of the wealth and fulness of final
mastery."

In "The Marbles of Ægina" Pater discusses the
quality of the beautiful group of sculpture discovered
in 1811 in a ruined temple of Athene in a remote part
of Ægina, and purchased for the Munich Gallery by
King Louis I. of Bavaria. The interest of this group
is that it seems the consummate flower of Dorian as
opposed to Ionian art, dating probably from about
the time of Marathon.

Pater skilfully contrasts the Ionian tendency of
thought—the brilliant, diffused, undirected play of
imagination, its restless versatility, its extreme indi-
vidualism—with the Dorian influence of severe sys-
tematisation, the subordination of the individual to the
state ; the group has the characteristics of the purest
Greek chivalry ; he shows the " dry earnestness " of the
craftsman, " with a sort of hard strength in detail, a
scrupulousness verging on stiffness, like that of an
early Flemish painter," and withal " his still youthful
sense of pleasure in the experience of the first rudi-
mentary difficulties of his art overcome."

"In this monument, . . ." he says, "pensive and visionary

as it may seem, those old Greek knights live with a truth like
that of Homer or Chaucer. In a sort of stiff grace, combined
with a sense of things bright or sorrowful directly felt, the
Æginetan workman is as it were the Chaucer of Greek
sculpture."

In the last of the *Studies*, "The Age of Athletic
Prizemen," composed twenty years later than the
earliest essays, Pater traces the effect of the athletic
system of Greece upon their sculpture. The pride of
health, of perfect agility, of graceful movement, all
concentrated upon the end in view, the perfect balance
of mind and body alike—these were the ends which
that system had in view—how different from our own
gloomy and commercial athletics !

The pride of the sculptor was to combine the
mystery of motion and of rest, to seize a moment
of intense energy—"the twinkling heel and ivory
shoulder" of the runner, "the tense nerve and full-
flushed vein," and to set it for ever in the imperishable
stillness of art. And further, behind the suppleness,
the delicate muscularity, the unspoiled freshness of
youth, to imprint if possible the mark of true
humanity upon those figures, the kind and simple
heart, the modest smile, the stainless purity of soul.
And again, in those funeral monuments of young
creatures snatched away before their time, to comfort
the mourner by some hint of the dignity, the tranquillising secret of death.

Pater takes the work of Myron and of Polycleitus as
the perfect expression of humanity—"humanity, with
a glowing, yet restrained joy and delight in itself, but
without vanity ; and it *is* pure."

"To have achieved just that," he writes, "was the Greek's
truest claim for furtherance in the main line of human development. He had been faithful, we cannot help saying . . .

in the culture, the administration, of the visible world ; and he
merited, so we might go on to say—he merited Revelation,
something which should solace his heart in the inevitable
fading of that."

It is here, perhaps, that the deepest value of these
Studies lies. Pater penetrates by patient skill, by
ardent sympathy, the glowing, simple, straightforward
life of the old world, with its light-hearted mirth,
its swift acquiescence in things as they are.

But he realises throughout that it is over and gone ;
that we cannot win it back ; but that it may cheer
and enlarge our view of life, our admiration for those
sunny spaces of history, if we can but apprehend it ;
and that we may win from it some tranquillity, some
brightness of spirit, which may fall on our heavier
hearts, our bewildered sophisticated minds, like fresh
winds blowing over the hills from the gates of the
morning. That it cannot wholly satisfy us he has no
doubt ; but that it may enliven and widen our minds
he is not less assured.

Up to this date Pater's work had been critical ; it
has been pointed out that it was never purely critical,
but a species of poetical and interpretative criticism, of
a creative order, working upon slender hints and employing artistic productions as texts and *motifs* for
imaginative creation.

But he now began to feel the impulse to produce
original creative work, and to use his own impressions,
his experiences, his speculations as material for imaginative treatment.

His only critical work for the next three years consisted of the essay on "Charles Lamb" which we have
already considered, a slight Shakespearian essay on
"Love's Labours Lost," and three of the *Greek Studies*.
But the year 1878 is memorable for the first appearance

of one of his most beautiful works, the one, in fact, which can be recommended to any one unacquainted with Pater's writings, as exhibiting most fully his characteristic charm.

The Child in the House is the sweetest and tenderest of all Pater's fancies, the work, we may say, where his art approached most nearly to a kind of music. We have before indicated the autobiographical vein of the piece, but it remains to say something of the art of the essay, which is conceived in a certain golden mood of retrospect, and makes an appeal to all who, however rarely, indulge a train of gentle recollection. Such a mood is wrought in us by a sort of sudden charm; the sight of old places where we have lived untroubled days brings it back with a wistful swiftness, so that we feel a yearning desire, it may be, for our own unstained past; we contrast what we are and what we have become, with what we were and with what we might have been. This mood, a sort of "death in life" as Tennyson says, may surprise natures overlaid with conventionalism and even coarseness. It is one of the commonest and most forcible, because truest, effects of pathos, in books that aim at dramatic effect, when the crust of later careless habit suddenly breaks, and the old clear stream of life seems to be running there below all the while.

Such an experience may hold within it, even for the most worldly and hardened minds, a hope of immortality, a hope of redemption. That strange and yearning hunger of the heart for a purity, a simplicity which it once had, before the bitter root of evil sent up its poisonous flowers into the soul, is one of the most primal emotions of nature. It is in such a mood that a man is apt to feel most self-forgiving, most self-pitying, because he feels that it is circumstance and seduction of sense that have marred a nature that in itself desired purity and simplicity. It is not perhaps the highest of emotions, because it is a mood in which life would seem to hold no lessons but the lesson of inevitable decline, ungenerous deterioration; but there is no denying its strength, its sad charm.

In *The Child in the House* we see a boy deeply sensitive to beautiful impressions, to all the quiet joys, the little details of home: its carved balusters and shadowy angles, its scents and sounds, its effects of light and shade, and further abroad, the trees of the garden, the hawthorn bush, with its "bleached and twisted trunk and branches" . . . with the fresh bloom—"a plumage of tender crimson fire out of the heart of the dry wood"—the shops of the city hard by, the belfry with its giddy winding stair,—"half, tint and trace and accident of homely colour and form, from the wood and the bricks; half, mere soul-stuff, floated thither from who knows how far."

And then, too, we see the child's love for the outward forms of religion; "the comely order of the sanctuary, the secrets of its white linen, and holy vessels, and fonts of pure water; and its hieratic purity and simplicity became the type of something he desired always to have about him in actual life. He pored over the pictures in religious books, and knew by heart the exact mode in which the wrestling angel grasped Jacob, how Jacob looked in his mysterious sleep, how the bells and pomegranates were attached to the hem of Aaron's vestment, sounding sweetly as he glided over the turf of the holy place."

Over this quiet and untroubled mood the shadow creeps. The boy begins to feel the touch of sorrow, of loss, of bereavement—the shadow of death. A cry heard on the stairs tells how the news of a death comes home to an aged heart; the little household pet, the Angora cat, sickens and dies, the tiny soul flickering away from the body; the young starling is caught and caged, but the boy cannot resist the cries of the mother-bird, the "sharp bound of the prisoner up to her nest-lings," and lets the sorrowing creature go.

One realises with a painful intensity with what a shock of bewildered emotion Pater must have realised as a child the first lessons of mortality, "the contact," as he wrote long afterwards, "of childhood with the great and inevitable sorrows of life, into which children can enter with depth, with dignity, and sometimes with a kind of simple, pathetic greatness, to the discipline of the heart."

Yet in this region there falls a certain vein of what may be called *macabre*, which might be thought morbid were it not obviously so natural—a dwelling on the accidents of mortality, the gradations of decay.

"He would think of Julian, fallen into incurable sickness, as spoiled in the sweet blossom of his skin like pale amber, and his honey-like hair; of Cecil, early dead, as cut off from the lilies, from golden summer days, from women's voices; and then what comforted him a little was the thought of the turning of the child's flesh to violets in the turf above him."

There is very little of human emotion in the vision; little dwelling upon companionship and near affections and relationships; and this is true to nature. The child whose nature is thus sensuously perceptive is often so much taken up by mere impression, by the varied, the enchanting outsides of things, the curious forms, the play of colour, the ray of sunlight like gold-dust, the light cast up from the snow upon the ceilings of rooms, that there is little leisure, little energy, to give to the simple affections of life. In this the picture is perfectly faithful ; the writer, by a sincerity of retrospect, has avoided the temptation to read into the childish spirit the emotions of the expanding heart ; it is all seen in the region of Maiden-sense, in the desirable clear light of the early morning, before the passionate impulses awake, before the intellect expands. Thus the pure art of the conception lies in the picturing the perfect isolation of the childish soul—not a normal soul, it must be remembered,—though perhaps the haunted emphasis of the style, its luxurious cadence, its mellowing of outline may tend to disguise from us how real and lifelike indeed, how usual an experience, is being recorded.

And for the style itself, it is a perfect example of a kind of poetical prose ; there is no involution, no intricacy. The language is perfectly simple ; and though some may feel a lusciousness, an over-ripeness of phrase to predominate, yet the effect is perfectly deliberate, and it is by the intention that we must judge it. It may be set in a paradise of floating melodies in which the brisk, the joyful, the energetic may be loath to linger ; yet for all who love the half-lit regions of the spirit, the meditative charm of things, *The Child in the House* must remain one of the purest pieces of word-melody in the language, and one of the most delicate characterisations of a mood that comes to many, and always with a secret and wistful charm.

Before we speak of *Marius the Epicurean*, which began to absorb Pater's energies from 1878 onwards, it will be as well to trace the slender thread of events. How uneventful his academical progress was may be augured from the fact that the year 1880 was in some ways almost the most momentous year of his life,

because it was in the course of it that Pater determined to resign the tutorship of the college. This step
meant a serious loss of income; but he was now embarked upon the task of constructing *Marius*, and could
no longer disguise from himself the fact that writing
was indubitably the most serious preoccupation of his
life. He saw that it was becoming impossible for him
to discharge the duties of the post adequately, and at
the same time carry on his literary work effectively.
The governing body of the college fully concurred in
his decision; and though the incident at first caused
Pater some pain, realising, as he did, that the feeling of
the society did not endorse his own theory of the functions of the tutorial office, yet he soon grew to perceive
that his resignation had been a blessing in disguise:
it freed him from work which was not particularly
congenial, work which needed qualities, such as a brisk
directness of address, a good-humoured strictness, a
businesslike determination, which Pater had never even
professed to possess. He continued to lecture; but he
was set free from the constant petty inroads on his time,
to which a college tutor is always liable, and from perpetual small engagements and interruptions. It is a
matter of regret that Pater did not realise this earlier.
He would both have saved himself some chagrin, and
he would have been able to give some of his best and
most vigorous years to what was after all the real
work of his life. There are, and always will be, abundance of effective college tutors who could not write
Marius the Epicurean; and, on the other hand, it is not
an agreeable or dignified thing for a great man of
letters, and a man, too, of a peculiarly sensitive temperament, to discover that he has been holding a post
which has not been regarded as by any means appropriate to his disposition, and that his discharge of its

duties, though at the cost of much patient effort and constant strain to himself, has not wholly satisfied his colleagues.

On the other hand, lecturing was always a congenial task to Pater. He spent much time and thought upon his lectures, and prepared them with such thoroughness and care, that he tended to over-elaborate them, thus impairing their value as orally delivered discourses, intended for immediate comprehension.

Mr. Humphry Ward writes :—

"I became a Fellow of Brasenose early in 1869, and for the next three years saw Pater almost daily. The common stories of him, at Tutors' meetings, scholarship elections, etc., are not far from the truth. He saw that other people were better fitted than he to arrange details ; but he did the work assigned to him very well, and with much labour. The only time I remember seeing him really angry was one night in Common Room when X., an elderly man and a former tutor, not over-burdened with ideals, made some cutting remark about the short hours and light work of modern lecturers. Pater, who had by that time had some five years' experience, and whose lectures (over the heads of most men) were crammed with thought and work, 'let himself go' in a series of the most bitter repartees about the perfunctory stuff of the older time, the shams, conventions, and orthodox impostures of X. and his contemporaries. Relations between them were afterwards strained."

In one college office, however, which Pater held until his death, he took great delight. The post of Dean is an almost honorary one, and the only official duty attached to it is that of presenting men for their degrees ; but it gives the holder a dignified stall, that on the extreme right, on the *decani* side, next to the altar, a stall dignified by a special canopy and an exalted desk. Pater never failed to occupy his stall both on Sunday morning and evening ; and he was a

strong advocate for the Sunday services being com-
pulsory. He said with truth that there were many
men who would be glad to have the habit of attending,
but who would fail to attend, especially on Sunday
mornings, partly from the attraction of breakfast
parties, or possibly from pure indolence, unless there
was a rule of attendance. As a matter of fact attendance was made a matter of individual taste, but
Pater continued to deplore it.

The service at Brasenose retains several peculiar
little ceremonies; the candles are lit at celebrations.
The Junior Fellows bring in the elements with
solemnity from the ante-chapel. When the procession
leaves the altar, the dignitaries who carry the alms and
the vessels bow at the lectern to the altar, and to the
Principal as they pass his stall. The Vice-Principal
bows to the altar on leaving his stall, and to the
Principal as he passes out. These little observances,
dating from Laudian or even pre-Reformation times,
were very congenial to Pater; and it was always
observed that though kneeling was painful to him, he
always remained on his knees, in an attitude of deep
reverence, during the whole administration of the
Sacrament. Indeed his reverent and absorbed appearance in chapel will be long remembered by those to
whom he was a familiar figure. His large pale face, his
heavy moustache and firm chin, his stoop, his eyes
cast down on his book in a veritable *custodia oculorum*—
all this was deeply impressive, and truly reflected the
solemn preoccupation which he felt. It is characteristic
of him that he used to regret that the ardour with
which the undergraduates sang the Psalms abated in
the *Magnificat*, which to him was the Song of Songs.

One of the very few pieces of writing composed
during the years devoted to *Marius* was the little

Essay on "Dante Gabriel Rossetti." This was written in 1883, not long after the poet's death, and is perhaps tinged with a memorial respect. Yet it is a subtle piece of praise, in which at the same time Pater seems delicately to weigh and test the author he is discussing; but one cannot help feeling that the innermost world of mystical passion in which Rossetti lived was as a locked and darkened chamber to Pater. He can look into it, he can admire the accessories of the scene, he can analyse, he can even sympathise to a degree; but it was after all to Pater an unnatural region; the heated atmosphere of passion, the supreme significance of love, being foreign and almost antipathetic to Pater's serious and sober view of intellectual tranquillity. To be intellectually and perceptively impassioned indeed he desired; but the physical ardours of love, the longing for enamoured possession—with this Pater had nothing in common.

He divined the truth indeed by a sort of analogy of sympathy.

"To Rossetti," he wrote, "life is a crisis at every moment. A sustained impressibility towards the mysterious conditions of man's everyday life, towards the very mystery itself in it, gives a singular gravity to all his work : those matters never became trite to him."

And again :—

" For Rossetti, then, the great affections of persons to each other, swayed and determined, in the case of his highly pictorial genius, mainly by that so-called material loveliness, formed the great undeniable reality in things, the solid resisting substance, in a world where all beside might be but shadow. The fortunes of those affections—of the great love so determined; its casuistries, its languor sometimes ; above all, its sorrows ; its fortunate or unfortunate collisions with those other great matters ; how it looks, as the long day of life goes

round, in the light and shadow of them : all this, conceived
with an abundant imagination, and a deep, a philosophic,
reflectiveness, is the matter of his verse."

This is ingenious enough, though it is hard to see
exactly what Pater meant by the "casuistry," the
"philosophical" vein of Rossetti. Rossetti rather
seems to feel, to state the problem, with the solution
of which philosophical minds might concern themselves.
Thus he affords plentiful matter for philosophical
speculation, but without philosophical intention ; and
indeed the deep-seated impatience of Rossetti's nature
had very little that was akin to the philosophical
spirit. He felt the mystery, which is the basis of
all philosophy, deeply ; but it was to him a baffling,
a despairing mystery ; not an attractive mystery,
supremely worth disentangling.

And thus it is that Pater chooses as the typical instance of Rossetti's work the single composition which
he says he would select if he had to name one to a
reader desiring to make acquaintance with him for the
first time—*The King's Tragedy*, a ballad which is hardly
typical of Rossetti at all, a piece of somewhat languid
unemotional workmanship ; with an excellence of its
own indeed, but not even touched with the inner spirit
of Rossetti's work. The reason of this is that Pater,
admiring with a deep respect and regard the attitude
of Rossetti to art, but yet not entering into his inner
mood, found the restraint, the directness, the absence
of exotic suggestiveness displayed in this poem more
congenial to him ; and thus the essay remains rather a
tour de force than a sympathetic appreciation ; he was
surveying Rossetti from the outside, not, as in the
writers whom he himself selected to deal with, from
the inside. Pater in his critical work bears always,
like the angel of the Revelation, a golden reed to

measure the city; but in this particular essay it is a piece of measuring and no more; and nothing could more clearly show the impersonal, the intellectual trend of Pater's temperament than his comparative failure to accompany Rossetti into the penetralia of his beauty-haunted and beauty-tortured spirit.

CHAPTER IV

MARIUS THE EPICUREAN

WHEN or how Pater began to form the design of *Marius the Epicurean* is not known. I cannot help doubting whether it was at first intended to be so large a work. His method of working was so elaborate, so deliberate, that he preferred shorter studies, episodes rather than continuous narrative. The year 1878 had been a more or less busy year. *The Child in the House* had appeared, and he had written three other studies; but he fell into a long silence. In 1879 nothing appeared from his pen. In 1880 two short Greek Studies were all that he published; in 1881 and 1882 he published nothing; in 1883 came the little study of Rossetti, published as an introduction in Ward's *English Poets*. In 1884 he published nothing; and at last in 1885 appeared *Marius the Epicurean*. It may be said that he gave up six years of his life, when his mental powers were at their strongest, to the preparation of this great book. He felt the strain imposed upon him by the size of the conception very severely ; moreover, he realised that to execute a subject on so large a scale was not wholly consonant with the bent of his mind; thus he wrote to Miss Paget (Vernon Lee) in July 1883 :—

"I have hopes of completing one half of my present chief work—an Imaginary Portrait of a peculiar type of mind in the

time of Marcus Aurelius, by the end of this vacation. . . . I
am wishing to get the whole completed, as I have visions of
many smaller pieces of work, the composition of which would
be actually pleasanter to me. However, I regard this present
matter as a sort of duty. For you know I think that there is
a . . . sort of religious phase possible for the modern mind,
the conditions of which phase it is the main object of my
design to convey."

So few personal hints are preserved of Pater's feelings
about any of his works that this statement, made in
the very throes of his labour, has a peculiar interest.

The motive of *Marius* is the tracing of the history
of a highly intellectual nature, with a deep religious
bias, through various stages of philosophy to the
threshold of Christianity; for it is impossible to
resist the conviction that Marius, dying technically
a Christian, his last moments soothed with Christian rites, would, if the creator of the book had de-
cided to prolong his progress, have become a professed
Christian.

Before we examine the book in detail we may briefly
indicate the stages through which Marius passes. The
first part traces his boyhood and school life, and
shows him, so to speak, in the orthodox stage, accept-
ing without question and with deep devotion the old
native religion of his land; in his school days comes the
mental awakening, and the birth of philosophical speculation. In the second part Marius takes his bearings, and becomes an intellectual Epicurean, of the
Cyrenaic school. He goes to Rome, and joins the
Imperial household as secretary to the Emperor Aurelius; and thus the Stoic position is brought before him
in its most attractive form. In the third part Marius
learns the inadequacy of his Cyrenaic philosophy, and
begins to see that there is an isolation and a lack of

sympathy in his position. He feels, too, the incompleteness of the Stoical system; and realises the need of a vital faith in some unseen and guiding power to preserve the serenity of mind which he desires. At the end of this part Marius is a Theist; at this point some unrecorded years are supposed to elapse. In the fourth part Marius is brought into direct contact with Christianity, but the appeal that it makes to him is mainly aesthetic; yet the faith in an unseen power comes nearer as the shadow of death begins to fall.

The background, carefully selected by Pater for the story to enact itself in, is the time of the Emperor Marcus Aurelius, a skilfully chosen period, when philosophy was fashionable, and when a liberal toleration was extended to Christianity; so that the development of Marius' philosophical and religious position takes place equably and naturally, without the severe strain which a period of barbarism or persecution might have put upon it.

It may also be observed that the story, though in a sense romantic, is free from emotional incidents. Two friendships play their part in the development of Marius; but there is no hint from first to last of the distracting emotion of love. With the exception of the faint picture of his mother in the opening of the book, transitory glimpses of the Empress Faustina and of the Christian widow Cecilia, there is an entire absence of the feminine element.

The book bears from first to last a strong personal, almost autobiographical impress; but at the same time it may be said that it is essentially a learned book; the local colour, the archaeological element, is very closely studied, and used, as was ever Pater's way, in no pedantic fashion, but fused with a perfect naturalism into the story. It is probably, however, true to say that the fact that Pater's knowledge of Italy was to a great extent superficial helped him to make his picture so clear and vivid; he was always at his best when he was amplifying slender hints and recollected glimpses. Too great a wealth of detailed materials tended, as we shall have occasion to observe in a later book, *Gaston de Latour*, to blur the sharp outline and to interfere with lucid execution.

The workmanship of the book is from first to last perfect; if there is a fault, and it may be fairly reckoned a fault, it lies in the introduction of certain rather over-lengthy episodes of translated or adapted passages, such as the story of Cupid and Psyche out of the *Golden Book of Apuleius*, the discourses of the Emperor Aurelius, and the conversation between Lucian and Hermotimus in the fourth part. In themselves they are models of literary grace; but in a connected narrative they are rather as wide trenches dug across the reader's path. They are felicitous indeed, and in a sense apposite; but just as in the *Arabian Nights* the device of story within story, like those nests of enamelled Indian boxes, causes a reluctant suspension of thought, so it may be said in *Marius* that the holding up of the main interest by the introduction of pieces of work on so minute a scale is not justified. It is as though pilgrims on a river, who desire above all things to complete their journey, should be compelled to traverse and explore a backwater, where no amount of beautiful detail reconciles them to the temporary abandonment of their original quest.

The art of the writer is perhaps most manifest in the first part, in which there is a delighted, a luxurious zest, hardly maintained in the same evenness throughout. Indeed, in spite of the size of the whole conception, and the perfect craftsmanship displayed, one is tempted to believe that Pater's real strength was the strength of the essayist rather than of the narrator ; a belief in which, as we have seen, he himself concurred.

In the first part is brought out with exquisite grace the life of the old Roman villa, buried in the remote countryside, near the sea : the name of the place is White-nights (*Ad Vigilias Albas*). It is half-farm, half-villa ; here the lonely boy grows up, with his widowed mother, whose life is but a life of shadowy sentiment consecrated to the memory of the dead.

"The little glazed windows in the uppermost chamber framed each its dainty landscape—the pallid crags of Carrara, like wildly twisted snow-drifts above the purple heath ; the distant harbour with its freight of white marble going to sea ; the lighthouse temple of *Venus Speciosa* on its dark headland, amid the long-drawn curves of white breakers. . . . The air there had always a motion in it, and drove the scent of the new-mown hay along all the passages of the house."

There is a beautiful passage about the boy's simple pursuits :—

"The ramble to the coast, over the marsh with its dwarf roses and wild lavender, and delightful signs, one after another—the abandoned boat, the ruined flood-gates, the flock of wild birds—that one was approaching the sea ; the long summer-day of idleness among its vague scents and sounds."

The house itself has the perfect Italian charm :—

"Lying away from the white road, at the point where it began to decline somewhat steeply to the marsh-land below. The building of pale red and yellow marble, mellowed by age . . . beyond the gates, was indeed but the exquisite fragment of a once large and sumptuous villa. Two centuries of the play of the sea-wind were in the velvet of the mosses which lay along its inaccessible ledges and angles. Here and there the marble plates had slipped from their places, where the delicate weeds had forced their way."

The boy grows up in an intense meditative cloistered mood, with a scrupulous conscience carefully fostered by his mother. "A white bird, she told him once, looking at him gravely, a bird which he must carry in his bosom across a crowded public place—his own soul was like that!" There is a traditional, inherited priesthood in the family, and the boy has a deep liturgical and ritual preoccupation; he is happiest in sacred places, and is conscious all his life, even in the midst of worldly distractions, of "a sort of hieratic beauty and order in the conduct of life." Perhaps it may be said that the ritual element, the pleasure in processions, and ordered hymns, and ceremonies and symbols is a little over-weighted. There is a sense of unreality, a lack of lifelikeness about the dramatic intentness with which the functions described are carried out; the devout temper of the central figure, of Marius himself, is too definitely presupposed in the worshippers. We shall have occasion to advert to this point again; but in this first part the spectacle of the religious ceremonies so tenderly and quaintly described gives one the feeling that one is watching the movements of the well-drilled *supers* of a play, rather than the unconstrained movement of actual life.

The boy's religious sense is deepened by a visit that he pays, for the sake of curing a boyish ailment, to a neighbouring temple of Aesculapius, where he listens to the mystical discourse of a young priest. He is shown through a sliding panel a retired long-drawn valley, lit with sunlight and closed by a misty mountain, which

gives him a strong sense of the unsuspected presence
of the unseen in life.   His mother dies; and he himself goes to Pisa to school, where he lives a somewhat
isolated life, with dreams of literary fame.

"While all the heart (of his fellow-scholars) was in their
limited boyish race, and its transitory prizes, he was already
entertaining himself, very pleasurably meditative, with the tiny
drama in action before him, as but the mimic, preliminary
exercise for a larger contest, and already with an implicit
epicureanism."

His view of life is coloured by an intense boyish
attachment to a school friend Flavian, a wayward, self-
absorbed, brilliant boy, with a strong taste for euphu-
istic literature, and of sceptical tendency.   Flavian's
life is already tainted by sensuality : "How often, afterwards, did evil things present themselves in malign
association with the memory of that beautiful head,
and with a kind of borrowed sanction and charm in its
natural grace!"   But Marius by a certain coldness
and fastidiousness of temperament preserves his purity
untouched.   And Marius here learns his first lessons in
Epicureanism of the higher kind.   "He was acquiring
what it is the chief function of all higher education to
impart, the art, namely, of so relieving the ideal or
poetic traits, the elements of distinction, in our everyday life—of so exclusively living in them—that the unadorned remainder of it, the mere drift or *débris* of our
days, comes to be as though it were not."   But it was
not the prescribed studies of the school that gave him
his hints of beauty.   "If our modern education, in its
better efforts, really conveys to any of us that kind of
idealising power, it does so (though dealing mainly,
as its professed instruments, with the most select and
ideal remains of ancient literature) oftenest by truant

reading; and thus it happened also, long ago, with
Marius and his friend."

Then comes Marius' literary training in association
with Flavian. He learns to appreciate the delicate
manipulation of words, the sharp impression, the exclusion of all "that was but middling, tame, or only half-
true," the refinement of what is already refined, the
fastidious correctness of form, the principle that
"to know when one's self is interested, is the first
condition of interesting other people." And this
brings Marius to the knowledge of the necessity of
scrupulous independence in literary taste.

"It was a principle, the forcible apprehension of which
made him jealous and fastidious in the selection of his intellectual food; often listless while others read or gazed
diligently; never pretending to be moved out of mere com-
plaisance to other people's emotions : it served to foster in
him a very scrupulous literary sincerity with himself. And
it was this uncompromising demand for a matter, in all
art, derived immediately from lively personal intuition, this
constant appeal to individual judgment, which saved his
euphuism, even at its weakest, from lapsing into mere
artifice."

Then comes the sudden death of Flavian, in a fever ;
and his end is told with a pathetic intensity which makes
it one of the strongest passages in the book. Flavian
is writing a poem, and struggles to continue his work
through the slow progress of decay. In this beautiful
passage one entirely false note is struck ; and it has a
special interest because it is the only moment at which
the narrative form is interrupted for a moment by the
dramatic. Marius lies down beside his dying friend,
heedless of possible contagion, to try and communicate
some warmth to the shivering frame. In the morning
Flavian's delirious anguish ceases with a revival of

mental clearness. " ' Is it a comfort,' Marius whispered then, ' that I shall often come and weep over you ? '— ' Not unless I be aware, and hear you weeping ! ' " It is certain that this effort to sum up a thought, which might have been present in Marius' mind, in definite words is an artistic mistake. If any confession of the terrible consciousness that death was at hand was to be made, it was for Flavian to confess it ; and Flavian's own answer is equally untrue to nature.

And so with the death of Flavian the first part closes in desolation.

The death of his friend is the event which, at the beginning of the second part, flings Marius into philosophical speculation. " To Marius . . . the earthly end of Flavian came like a final revelation of nothing less than the soul's extinction. Flavian had gone out as utterly as the fire among those still beloved ashes." Thus he is confronted in the sternest and saddest way with the mystery of death : and the thought comes home to him that he must at all costs realise the significance of life, and how he must play his part in the days that remain before he too passes into shadow and silence ; the religion of his childhood deserts him ; and he is forced to turn to the " honest action of his own untroubled, unassisted intelligence."

He secluded himself in a severe intellectual meditation, becoming something of a mystery to his fellows. He was reading, " for the most part, those writers chiefly who had made it their business to know what might be thought concerning that strange, enigmatic, personal essence, which had seemed to go out altogether, along with the funeral fires." He studies Heraclitus, and learns to mistrust habitual impressions and uncorrected sensation and to discern the movement in things of "the sleepless, ever-sustained, inexhaustible energy of the divine reason." He accepts the canon that the individual must be to himself the measure of all things, and resolves to limit his researches to what immediately interests him, resting peacefully in a profound ignorance of all beside. "He would entertain no theory of conduct which did not allow its due weight to this primary element of incertitude or negation, in the conditions of man's life." And here he fell under the dominion of Aristippus of Cyrene, who was the first to translate the abstractions of metaphysics into a practical sentiment. He, too, was more than half an agnostic; but instead of his agnosticism leading to a languid enervation, it led rather to a perpetual and inextinguishable thirst for experience.

"What Marius saw in him was the spectacle of one of the happiest temperaments coming, so to speak, to an understanding with the most depressing of theories"; and the practical conclusion he arrived at was that self-culture was probably the best solution, the impulse to "adorn and beautify, in scrupulous self-respect, our souls, and whatever our souls touch upon—these wonderful bodies, these material dwelling-places through which the shadows pass together for a while, the very raiment we wear, our very pastimes and the intercourse of society."

Aristippus, indeed, became to Marius a master of decorous and high-minded living. Metaphysic, as described by Michelet, "the art of bewildering oneself methodically," he must spend little time upon that. "Not pleasure, but a general completeness of life, was the practical ideal to which this anti-metaphysical metaphysic really pointed," and to acquire this, to regard life as the end of life, the only way was through "insight through culture, into all that the present moment holds in trust for us, as we stand so briefly in its presence."

The pursuit of vivid sensations and intellectual apprehensions must be his work, until such a manner of life, by its effort to live days "lovely and pleasant," might become a kind of hidden mystic religion. But there was no touch of hedonism in this :—

"Not pleasure, but fulness of life, and 'insight' as conducting to that fulness—energy, variety, and choice of experience, including noble pain and sorrow even, loves such as those in the exquisite old story of Apuleius, sincere and strenuous forms of the moral life . . . whatever form of human life, in short, might be heroic, impassioned, ideal : from these the 'new Cyrenaicism' of Marius took its criterion of values."

This would involve "a life of industry, of industrious study, only possible through healthy rule, keeping clear the eye alike of body and soul."

Marius then, with his creed formulated, at nineteen years of age, sets out for Rome, where he has an old family mansion, to become the amanuensis of the Emperor. There is a beautiful description of his journey : how the sun went down "though there was still a glow along the road through the shorn cornfields, and the birds were still awake about the crumbling gray heights of an old temple."

On the journey he meets the young Christian knight, Cornelius. And it must be here confessed that the youthful soldier of the Imperial guard, with his gilded armour, his blithe manliness, his sense of secret serenity, is one of the least convincing figures of the book. To put it in the plainest way possible, there is an indefinable taint of priggishness about Cornelius, and Pater in vain labours to create a charm about him. To weave such a charm the elabo-

rate narrative style is inadequate; one gets no glimpse
into the blithe and serene mind of Cornelius; he is
"faultily faultless, icily regular, splendidly null"—no
touch of humanity ever comes to relieve his statuesque
pose, and one wearies of his golden armour and his
handsome face.   Nothing but dramatic art, such as the
art of Scott, could have given Cornelius attractiveness;
and even he would have been baffled by the sober perfection of the young knight.   One longs that he should
lose his temper, make some human mistake, exhibit
some trace of emotion or even frailty; but he takes
instead his icy shining way through the story, and the
heart never desires to follow him.

Then comes Marius' first sight of Rome, his realisation of the fact that it was, beside being a city of palaces,
become the romantic home of the most restless religious
instinct, of the wildest superstition.   Religions were
draining into Rome, as the rivers into the sea.   In the
midst moved the stately figure of the Stoic Emperor,
whom Marius first sees in a religious procession, and
whose calm face, with its prominent eyes demurely
downcast, but yet "broadly and benignantly observant,"
candid gaze, and ascetic air, as though "the flesh had
scarcely been an equal gainer with the spirit," impressed him profoundly.   With him walked the
goodly, comely, sensual Lucius Verus, the other
Augustus, with his "strange capacity for misusing
the adornments of life, with a masterly grace."   Then
follows the Emperor's discourse on the Vanity of
Human Ambitions, delivered in the Senate, a skilful
cento of aphorisms taken from the *Meditations*, and
finally Marius' introduction to the Imperial household, his sight of Faustina the Empress, Fronto the
philosopher, and the Emperor himself.   He sees,
too, a gladiatorial show, at which the Emperor sits

impassibly, writing and reading, and wonders at the
tolerance, "which seemed to Marius to mark Aurelius
as his inferior now and for ever on the question of
righteousness ; to set them on opposite sides, in some
great conflict."

It may be freely confessed that Pater does con-
trive, by pathetic and emotional touches, to bring out
with wonderful vividness the human charm of the
Emperor, his deep patience, his fatigue, his affection-
ateness, his devotion to duty.   He and Flavian remain
as the two vital figures of the book, apart from the
hero himself ; and it may be held a true triumph of a
species of historical art to have evolved so real, so
dignified, so intensely vivid a figure out of the somewhat chilly abstractedness that had hitherto surrounded the philosophic Lord of legions, the Stoic
master of the world.

In the third part of *Marius*, which is much shorter
than any of the other parts, the revelation grows
more distinct.   Marius, overcome with doubt as to
whether his new intellectual scheme can be harmonised
with the old serious morality of his childhood, hears
a discourse by Fronto on the question of morals.

"He supposed his hearer to be, with all sincerity, in search
after some principle of conduct (and it was here that he
seemed to Marius to be speaking straight to him) which might
give unity of motive to an actual rectitude, a cleanness and
probity of life, determined partly by natural affection, partly
by enlightened self-interest or the feeling of honour, due in
part even to the mere fear of penalties. . . . How tenderly—
more tenderly than many stricter souls—he might yield himself to kindly instinct ! What fineness of charity in passing
judgment on others ! What an exquisite conscience of other
men's susceptibilities ! He knows for how much the manner,
because the heart itself, counts, in doing a kindness. He goes
beyond most people in his care for all weakly creatures ;

judging, instinctively, that to be but sentient is to possess rights. He conceives a hundred duties, though he may not call them by that name, of the existence of which purely duteous souls may have no suspicion. He has a kind of pride in doing more than they, in a way of his own."

And then the orator proceeds to sketch a kind of universal commonwealth, a heavenly citizenship, in which all men should realise their position, their duty ; and Marius falls to wondering whether there could be any such inner community of humanity, wider than even the community of nationality, and with a larger patriotism, with an aristocracy of elect spirits, an ever-widening example, and a comely order of its own. He realises that his Cyrenaicism is after all but an enthusiasm characteristic of youth, almost a fanaticism, and that something wider, larger, more impersonal is needed, as life goes on. He realised that in his first philosophy there had been "some cramping, narrowing, costly preference of one part of his own nature," and that he had paid a great price "in the sacrifice of a thousand possible sympathies" for the intense personal appreciation of the beauty of the moment. It was a narrow perfection that he had been aiming at after all, the perfection of "capacities of feeling, of exquisite physical impressions, of an imaginative sympathy." But he had rejected the wider, the more venerable system of religious sentiments and ideas, which had grown up in the vast field of human experience. And thus he saw that he could not stay where he was ; that he must recognise not only his own personal point of view, but the wider community of humanity.

In this frame of mind Marius has a memorable interview with the Emperor, who, in order to raise funds for the war, has determined to sell by public auction the accumulated treasures of the Imperial palace, and

is feeling with an austere joy the pleasure of a deep
philosophical detachment from the world.   Marius
sees that this kind of renunciation, a renunciation of
the very things of the purest quality of beauty that
his philosophy had taught him to value, may bring
with it a loftier and simpler kind of joy than even the
sober and refined enjoyment of them.   Aurelius, with
a supreme sense of duty, is about to plunge into the
uncongenial labours of a great campaign, and Marius
sees that in the selfless surrender to what appears the
Divine will lay his true generosity of soul.   He sees
that one of the strongest features of the Emperor's
character is the union of intellectual independence
with a tender sympathy for all the manifestations of
the popular religious sense, realising, as he does, that
men must reach their ideal by very different paths.
Marius finds, among the Emperor's papers committed
to him, a document, a species of diary, full of the most
intimate self-communings.   And in spite of the magnificence of character, the resolute determination, the
amazing generosity there revealed, there is a note of
heaviness.   He sees how "the forced and yet facile
optimism, refusing to see evil anywhere, might lack,
after all, the secret of genuine cheerfulness.   It left
in truth a weight upon the spirits; and with that
weight unlifted, there could be no real justification
of the ways of Heaven to man."   The cheerfulness
of demeanour, indeed, to which the Emperor had
attained, was not a spontaneous joy breaking out
from an inner source of happy faith, but a practised,
a deliberate attitude, attained by a rigorous self-
restraint.   Marius thinks of Cornelius, whose cheerfulness seems of a totally different kind, "united with
the bold recognition of evil as a fact in the world,"
yet he sees or suspects in Cornelius an irrepressible

and impassioned hopefulness. He finds it necessary
to go to Præneste, where the Emperor is staying for
a few days with his younger children, and arrives to
find the little Annius Verus dying; and here comes
one of the beautiful touches through which one comes
so close to the humanity of Aurelius :—

"He saw the emperor carry the child away—quite conscious
at last, but with a touching expression . . . of weakness and
defeat—pressed close to his bosom, as if he yearned just then
for one thing only, to be united, to be absolutely one with it,
in its obscure distress."

And so the Emperor sets out on the campaign from
which he has reason to think that he may never return.
The pageantry of his departure, the magnificent armour
that he wears, are in strange contrast to the face of
Aurelius, "with its habitually dejected hue grown
now to an expression of positive suffering." He de-
parts, and Marius returns to his musings ; but in a
lonely ride into the Sabine Hills he has a strange uplifting of spirit, in which he feels that behind all the
complexity of life, "behind the veil of a mechanical and
material order, but only just behind it," there moves
a guide, a heavenly friend, ever at his side, to whom
he is perhaps dearer than even to himself, a Father
of Men.

Marius felt that after the realisation of this possibility, his life could never be quite the same again,
and that only in the light of this hope could he apprehend the secret of the lonely pilgrimage upon which
he seemed to be bound.

Some time is now supposed to elapse, and in the
fourth part Marius comes upon the scene again at a
banquet at which the young Commodus is present,
and also the great Apuleius, with whom Marius has

a few moments of private conversation. Apuleius unfolds to his companion his belief in a kind of middle order of beings, between man and God, by whom the prayers and aspirations of humanity can be carried and interpreted to God. It is, indeed, the doctrine of the ministry of angels which is thus foreshadowed; and the effect on Marius is to give a heightened sense of unreality to the world in which he moves; and it is at this juncture that he visits with Cornelius the villa of Cecilia, and is deeply impressed with the order, the industry, the joyful peace of the household. Cornelius takes his friend through a garden and into the old catacomb of the Cecilii, where Marius sees the graves of Christians, and reads with a strange thrill of spirit the touching and inspiring inscriptions on their tombs, that seem to exorcise the terrors of death by a serene and lively hope. The fresh and cool sensation of peace with which the whole surroundings are invested is to Marius like a window opened from a hot and fragrant room into the dawn of some other morning. Here, he fancied, might be the cure, the anodyne for the deep sorrowfulness of spirit under which he seemed to have been always labouring. He began to discern the source of that untroubled serenity, that quiet happiness of which he had always been conscious in his friend. The Christian ideal of that period, during the peace of the Antonines, had lent itself to the harmonious development of human nature, in a due proportion, rather than to the idea of ascetic self-sacrifice; and the divine urbanity and moderation of this secluded household exercised a strong spell over the sensuous temperament of Marius.

But here there creeps in the intense liturgical and ritual preoccupation of the author. Marius goes to find Cornelius at the Cecilian villa, and becomes by accident the spectator of a solemn celebration of the Eucharistic mystery.

The description of the service is exquisitely, almost lusciously rendered ; it satisfies Marius' deep instinct for worship to the uttermost. But here the reader cannot help feeling a lack of proportion ; the sensuous element triumphs over the intellectual. The choir of children, the white-robed youths, the bishop himself, "moving the hands which seemed endowed in very deed with some mysterious power . . . or chanting in cadence of a grave sweetness the leading parts of the rite," have a certain unreality about them, an impossible peace, an almost mawkishness of conception. It seems, perhaps, a hard and unsympathetic criticism to make of a passage into which so much tender idealism has passed, but there is a taint as of the Sunday-school type about the incident, which not even its elaborate art can surmount. One feels in a false atmosphere, an atmosphere which is not only unrealisable but actually undesirable. It lacks the salt of humanity, and is touched with the unalloyed meekness which the manly heart, however tender, however responsive, does not really wish to enforce. The narrative then passes with a singular abruptness back to Marius' literary preoccupations ; and the intrusion of this chapter at this point may be held to be one of the few artistic mistakes of the book. It interrupts the progress, as if by a whimsical diversion, at a crucial point ; it introduces the figure of the satirist Lucian, and relates a conversation with Hermotimus, a beautiful thing in itself, but with no real bearing on the development of the central theme. The upshot of the talk, which is in itself a delicious Platonic dialogue, full of humour and fancy, is that there is no certain criterion of philosophical ideas, but that the adoption of any form of philosophical belief is dictated by a preference and an instinct in the disciple; Lucian, employing a species of Socratic questioning, extinguishes, by a sort of affectionate and tender scepticism, the burning enthusiasm of the boy's ardent philosophy. The real gist of the chapter lies in the sight which Marius has as he returns to Rome of a wayside crucifix; and the echoes of the conversation take shape in his mind, making him reflect whether it were possible that Love "in the greatness of his strength" could condescend to sustain Love "fainting by the road." It is just a hint, like a ray of light through a half-opened door.

There follow passages of a diary of Marius with many vignettes of small sorrowful and loving things; a racehorse led to death, a crippled child at play with his sister, a boy, the son of a labourer, waiting with his father's dinner, and gazing "with a sorrowful distaste for the din and dirt" at the brick-kiln where his father is at work. The *motif* of the chapter is that an enlarged charity, a passionate sympathy with humanity, so apt to be excluded by a philosophical system, contains perhaps a truer estimate of the secret of life.

"A protest comes, out of the very depths of man's radically hopeless condition in the world. . . . Dared one hope that there is a heart, even as ours . . . a heart even as mine, behind this vain show of things ! "

And now again Marius goes to the house of Cecilia, and sees the burial of a child; he notes that not even the intensity of human grief which the household feels and manifests in its stifled sobbing, its unrestrained tears, can do away with " the habitual gleam of joy, the placid satisfaction" of spirit. At the service is read

aloud an epistle speaking of martyrdoms in Gaul, of
Blandina and Ponticus, bringing to Marius the sense
of the "strange new heroism," uplifting sorrow out
of the region of "private regret," which seems to be
appearing in the world.

Marius sees the return of the Emperor in triumph;
and he is filled with a sense of sickening reaction at the
sight of the captives in the procession, and at the fact
that one of so lofty a spirit as the Emperor can fall so
low as to take his place in the midst of so barbarous a
ceremony. "Aurelius himself seemed to have under-
gone the world's coinage, and fallen to the level of his
reward, in a mediocrity no longer golden." And thus
at that moment the vital failure of the philosophical
attitude reveals itself to Marius; he sets out to revisit
his old home, with a shadow of approaching disaster
upon him. He opens the old mausoleum of the
house, and the thought that he may be the last of
his race, blending with a passionate tenderness for
the past, his father, his ancestry, induces him to
bury all the remains of the dead deep below the
ground.

" He himself watched the work, early and late ; coming on the
last day very early, and anticipating, by stealth, the last
touches, while the workmen were absent ; one young lad
only, finally smoothing down the earthy bed, greatly surprised at the seriousness with which Marius flung in his
flowers, one by one, to mingle with the dark mould."

And now the end comes with a certain unexpectedness.
Marius, reflecting on his own life, sees that though with
a natural bent for adventure and action, all his progress
has been inward and meditative, always aiming at
detachment rather than at the intermingling of himself
with the current.

The death that follows was no doubt designed by
the author to have something tragic and what may be
called almost sensational about it, to relieve by contrast
the contemplative texture of the work.   Cornelius finds
Marius in depression and weariness at White-nights,
and contrasting sadly his own languor of spirit with
the irrepressible youth of the other.

They set off for Rome.   The plague is ravaging the
land, and this, together with a shock of earthquake,
loosens the superstitions of the natives ; an attack is
made on a body of Christians who are praying by the
grave of the martyr Hyacinthus.   Blood is shed, and
the group, including Cornelius and Marius, are arrested
and sent for trial to the chief town of the district.
Marius, in obedience to a sudden instinct, procures the
liberation of Cornelius by bribing the guards, explain-
ing to Cornelius that he is allowed to depart to procure
the means of legal defence.   The first feeling of Marius
as he sees Cornelius depart is a kind of innocent pride
that he, who had always believed himself to lack the
heroic temper, could thus display a sudden courage.
But a mood of dark melancholy follows ; he foresees
that he will suffer the death of a common felon, without even the Christian consolation of the martyr's
example.   The hardships of the march bring on a
fever, and Marius is abandoned by the guard as a
dying man in a little hill village.   At first the rest
and quiet relieve his tortured mind, and he is filled
with a sense of gratitude to the unseen Friend who has
guarded him through his long journey, and draws near
in faith to the crucified Jesus.   In this half-peaceful
mood he finds himself able to think of death with an
intense and reverent curiosity, as of a door through
which he must pass to his further pilgrimage.   And
then the weariness comes back tenfold as death draws

near; the Christians of the place surround his bed, and hearing of the deed he has done in saving Cornelius, administer the last rites, the consecrated bread, the holy oil; and when all is over bury him with the accustomed prayers, and with an added joy, holding him to have been a martyr indeed.

Such is the progress of this melancholy and meditative soul, to whom even youth had hardly been a season of joy, so oppressed was it by the sad malady of thought.

It is difficult to treat so intimate a memorial of a personality in a critical spirit; and we may say at once that to deal with a book that is so sacred a document in the spirit of finding fault with it for not being other than it is, is wholly out of place. It may be said to have nothing heroic about it, but to be almost purely spectatorial. It may be easily labelled introspective, even morbid; but it is of the very essence of the book that it is designed to trace the story of a soul to which the ordinary sources of happiness are denied, and to which, from temperament and instinct, the whole of life is a species of struggle, an attempt to gain serenity and liberty by facing the darkest problems candidly and courageously, rather than by trying to drown the mournful questionings of the mind in the tide of life and activity. What we have to do is, granted the type and the conception, to see how near the execution comes to the idea which inspired it.

It will be seen that the book is to a certain extent the history of a noble failure; Marius' attempt to arrive, by his own unassisted strength, by a firm and candid judgment, at a solution for life, breaks down at every point. He falls back in a kind of weariness upon the old religious intuitions that had been his joy in boyhood. He learns that not in isolation, not in self-

sufficiency, does the soul draw near to the apprehension
of the truth, but in enlarged sympathy, in the sense of
comradeship, in the perhaps anthropomorphic instinct
of the Fatherhood, the brotherhood of God.   It is a
passionate protest not only against materialism, but
against the intellectual ideal too ; it is a no less passionate pronouncement of the demand of the individual to
be satisfied and convinced, within his brief span of life,
of the truth that he desires and needs.

But the weakness of the case is, that instead of
emphasising the power of sympathy, the Christian
conception of Love, which differentiates Christianity
from all other religious systems, Marius is after all
converted, or brought near to the threshold of the
faith, more by its sensuous appeal, its liturgical
solemnities ; the element, that is to say, which Christianity has in common with all religions, and which is
essentially human in character.   And more than that,
even the very peace which Marius discerns in Christianity is the old philosophical peace over again.
What attracts Marius in the Christian spirit is its
serenity and its detachment, not its vision of the
corporateness of humanity and the supreme tie of
perfect love.   This element is introduced, indeed, but
fitfully, and as if by a sense of historical fidelity,
rather than from any personal conviction of its
supreme vitality.   With all its candid effort the spirit
of the writer could not disentangle itself from the
sense of personal isolation, of personal independence ;
there is no sense of union with God : the soul and its
creator, however near they draw in a species of divine
sympathy, are always treated of as severely apart and
separate.   The mystical union of the personality with
God is outside the writer's ken ; the obedience of the
human will to the divine, rather than the identification

of the two, is the end to which he moves; and this
perhaps accounts for the drawing of the line at the
point which leaves Marius still outside the fold, because one feels that the author himself hardly dared
to attempt to put into words what lay inside.

And now, as our chief concern is with the literary
art of the book, we may turn to consider its main
characteristics.

"Though the manner of his work," says Pater, speaking
of Marius, "was changed formally from poetry to prose, he
remained, and must always be, of the poetic temper: by
which, I mean, among other things, that quite independently
of the general habit of that pensive age he lived much, and as
it were by system, in reminiscence."

This is true of the book itself: we cannot say that
it is all reminiscence, but it is all bound up with
reminiscence. The author makes little attempt to
deal with the fresh atmosphere, the sharp detail of the
present; still less to throw himself forward into the
glowing idealisation of the future; the whole book is
that of a man looking back, the outlines of what he
sees all mellowed and rounded in a sort of golden haze
of pensive light. And it is thus essentially poetical.
The carefully studied archaeology of the book is never
insisted upon, but only used as contributing a pictur-
esque and hinted background; but it is poetical in the
sense that there is no attempt at definite or scientific
statement—even the abstrusest doctrines of philosophy, as well as the intricate details of the setting,
are all touched with a personal appeal. Nothing is
presented in its own dry light; it is all coloured,
tinged, transformed by the mind of the writer, it all
ministers to his mood.

The one artistic fault of the book is, as we have said,

the introduction of alien episodes, of actual documents into the imaginary fabric; and these give the effect, so to speak, of pictures hung upon a tapestry. The style is of course entirely individual; it is a style of which Pater was the inventor; it is not only easy to imitate, but it is almost impossible, if one studies it closely, not to fall into the very mannerisms of the writer. Of course it is easy to say that it is languid, highly perfumed, luscious, over-ripe; but here again we fall into the error of analysing the essential quality, and disapproving of it. It cannot be pretended that it is brisk, lucid, or lively; there is nothing of "sonorous metal, blowing martial sounds," about it; rather it winds like a cloud of smoke on a still day, hanging in fine-drawn veils and aerial weft. It is intensely deliberate, self-conscious, mannerised. Its fault is to fall into involved sentences, with long parentheses and melodious cadences. It never trips or leaps or runs; but always moves like a slow pontifical procession, stiff-robed, mystical, and profound. It never aims at crisp precision, but rather at a subtle refinement, a mysterious grace.

Its finest art is displayed in an economy of impression, whose very severity ends in a suggestiveness of picture which is attained, not by elaborate description, but by haunted glimpses of beauty. These touches of perfect loveliness relieve the graver analysis with a sudden sense of coolness and repose, as a student may look up from a book into a sunny garden, and find in the golden light some hallowing, some confirmation, of the inner mood. And the most severe passages of philosophical writing are again lit up by exquisite similes or still more delicate metaphors, in which the whole sentence seems steeped and stained, as with the juice of a berry shut in upon the page.

H

Thus he writes :—

"He, too, paused at the apprehension of that constant motion of things—the drift of flowers, of little or great souls, of ambitious systems, in the stream around him, the first source, the ultimate issue, of which, in regions out of sight, must count with him as but a dim problem. . . . He might reserve it as a fine, high, visionary consideration, very remote upon the intellectual ladder, just at the point, indeed, where that ladder seemed to pass into the clouds, but for which there was certainly no time left just now by his eager interest in the real objects so close to him, on the lowlier earthy steps nearest the ground."

No one can say that these sentences are obvious, clear, sharply cut. But they are full of a poetical suggestiveness, and sparkle with hidden lights like opalescent gems.

Indeed, the writing of Pater may best be compared to the opal. It has not the clear facets, the limpid colour of the unclouded gem; but it is iridescent, rounded, shot with flashing lights and suffused with a milky mist of which one can hardly say whether it be near or far. It is this strange sense of depth, so inherent in a cloudy gem, that it gives one. One can measure to a millimetre the actual bulk of the jewel; but within that limit, what spent lights gleam, what misty textures roll! it is like a little coloured eyehole, through which one can discern the orbits of pale stars, the swimming vapours of some uncreated world.

But the fact is that most of the objections that can be urged against *Marius* are *prima facie* objections; it is criticised mostly for not possessing qualities that it was not meant to have; it stands as one of the great works of art of which it may be said that the execution comes very near to the intention. Possibly

CHAPTER V

LONDON LIFE

In 1885, the year of the publication of *Marius*, Pater made a change in his environment; he took a house in London, No. 12, Earl's Terrace, Kensington, near Holland House, which he held for eight years. This change of residence was dictated both by a desire for change, and by the feeling that the wider circle and more varied influences of London would lend him a larger and more vivid stimulus. He still resided during the term at Brasenose, and lived in London mostly in the vacations. Those who visited him in London were struck by the extreme quiet and simplicity of the household arrangements. Pater went a good deal into society, and enjoyed it greatly; but otherwise he just pursued his ordinary routine of writing and working as he might have done at Oxford. The London period was one of great interest and enjoyment; he found a warm welcome awaiting him in literary, artistic, and social circles; he made many new friends, and expanded in many directions.

In London, as at Oxford, there was never the least personal luxury in Pater's *ménage*, though there was quiet and solid comfort. His official income and the receipts from his books were practically all that he had to depend upon. He was fond of travelling, to the very end of his life, both in France and Italy. He generally went abroad for five or six weeks, and

always with his sisters. He liked the movement, the
gaiety, the greater *épanouissement* of France. He threw
himself with a deep appreciation into all that he saw,
and entered, as may be seen from his writings, with
a sympathetic intensity into the spirit of the buildings, the sculpture, the pictures, the landscapes that he
saw. He used also to tire himself, on these occasions,
with excess of walking, his only form of exercise. But
still, his enjoyment of travel may be best tested by the
fact that his favourite tonic for the slight weariness,
resulting perhaps from the emotional reaction, which
he experienced for a day or two after his return from
a tour, was to plan a scheme of travel for the following
year.

The years that followed were the most fruitful years
of Pater's life. The reception of *Marius* had been both
respectful and enthusiastic ; it had lifted its author
into a position in the very front rank of English prose-
writers. And then, too, the strain of the continuous
work was lifted off his shoulders, and he was able with
renewed zest to take up some of the many subjects
which in the course of those laborious years had
appealed to him as congenial. He had faithfully and
religiously eschewed the temptation to pursue them,
subordinating all vagrant fancies to his central theme ;
he could now expatiate freely ; moreover he had
found, in the course of his work, if not fluency, at all
events a pleasurable flow of appropriate if characteristic language. He began to contribute reviews to the
Guardian, the *Athenæum*, the *Pall Mall Gazette*. Some
twenty of these reviews have been identified, and
nine reviews which appeared in the *Guardian* have
been since reprinted, privately in 1896, and latterly
published 1901.

These reviews are not of very great intrinsic value ;

but evidently considerable time has been spent upon them; the book with which they deal has been carefully read, and a delicate appreciation composed. What strikes one most in reading them is, in the first place, a marked tenderness for the feelings of the author whom he is reviewing, and a great and princely generosity of praise. There seems to be no severity about Pater; and he enters into the intentions of the writer with a great catholicity of sympathy. There is also visible a certain irresponsible enjoyment about the tone of the reviews, as if with anonymity he had put on a certain gaiety to which in his public appearances he felt bound to be a stranger.

Of course no great originality is to be expected in these compositions. Thus reviewing three editions of Wordsworth in the *Guardian* of February 27, 1889, he does not hesitate to use many of his own deliberate dicta from the "Wordsworth" essay which had appeared in the *Fortnightly* in 1874, and was to be reprinted in the same year in which he wrote the review in question (1889) in *Appreciations*. Perhaps the review of *Robert Elsmere* (*Guardian*, March 28, 1888) reveals most plainly the almost childlike delight which Pater could take in the *motif* and characters of a story which one would have thought would not have been by any means congenial to him.

Pater's chief critical work in 1886 was the essay on Sir Thomas Browne, to be published afterwards in the *Appreciations* of 1889. In this study the same principle of autobiographical selection comes out which we see so constantly at work in Pater's mind. The charm for him in Browne is that whimsical mixture of scientific and poetical elements, the ceremonious piety, the strong sensitiveness to the human association of things, the thirst to record and express a point of view.

Again, what gives Pater a strong interest in Browne's writings is the fact that he exhibits at a remote point the evolution of native English prose, that evolution which was distracted, we would believe, by the wave of classicalism, the effect of the tide of the Renaissance, which beat, belated and enfeebled, on our solitary shores. The invasion of English prose by the wrong kind of classicalism, the sonorous elaboration of Latinity instead of the lucid charm of native English, deferred, no doubt, the development of natural English prose, though it perhaps eventually ministered to its richness. Browne, like Montaigne in France, is the type of the essayist, the writer whose object is not the precise statement of a case, but the saturation of a subject in his own personality. Such writing is often lacking in structure and conception, but it has an indefinable charm. "It has," writes Pater of Browne's style, "its garrulity, its various levels of painstaking, its mannerism, pleasant of its kind or tolerable, together with much, to us intolerable, but of which he was capable on a lazy summer afternoon down at Norwich." It is just that which is the charm ; that it brings before us the same elements that delight us in our own life, the summer, the freshness of the open air, the pleasant house with its gardens and studious chambers, together with a venerable setting which does but heighten the sense that though philosophical, political, and religious theories may have shifted and developed, the greater part of men's lives and joys are made up out of far simpler and commoner elements, which hardly indeed change from century to century.

And then, too, there comes in the art of the psychologist, "to whom all the world is but a spectacle in which nothing is really alien from himself, who has hardly a sense of the distinction between great and little among things that are at all, and whose half-pitying, half-amused sympathy is called out especially by the seemingly small interests and traits of character in the things or the people around him."

The other points in which the character of Browne appealed strongly to Pater are his emotional interest in ecclesiastical ceremony, which made him rejoice in the return of the comely Anglican order to the Norwich churches at the time of the Restoration, which caused him to weep abundantly at the sight of solemn processions; and there is also the vein of curious speculation about death, his anatomical and antiquarian researches alike testifying to his preoccupation with the thought of the mystery of decay and extinction of vital power; till his life becomes, as Pater says humorously, "too like a lifelong following of one's own funeral."

Pater brings out very clearly the fact that the *Religio Medici* is perhaps a misleading title. One would expect a treatise dealing with scientific analysis, tending naturally to materialism and scepticism, but struggling through and retaining a hold on religion, all the stronger for the speculative temptations that would seem to block the way. But Browne, says Pater, "in spite of his profession of boisterous doubt, has no real difficulties, and his religion, certainly, nothing of the character of a concession." He is a convinced Theist, and a confirmed pietist. "The *Religio Medici* is a contribution, not to faith, but to piety; a refinement and correction, such as piety often stands in need of; a help, not so much to religious belief in a world of doubt, as to the maintenance of the religious mood amid the interests of a secular calling." He goes further, indeed, and shows that it is only Browne's method, not

his mind, that is scientific. "What he is busy in the
record of, are matters more or less of the nature of
caprices; as if things, after all, were significant of their
higher verity only at random, and in a sort of sur-
prises, like music in old instruments suddenly touched
into sound by a wandering finger, among the lumber
of people's houses."

And thus, though Browne is in a sense an investi-
gator, he misses the conclusion to which his investiga-
tions are tending; because he does not really seek to
arrive at a conclusion, but only to harmonise facts, as
he investigates them, with a conclusion which he has
inherited rather than drawn.

Of the essay on "Feuillet's *La Morte*," the work of
the same year, it is unnecessary to speak. It is a mere
review, full of copious quotation, with a slender trickle
of exposition; Pater neither philosophises nor evolves
principles; he merely analyses the story; indeed, it is
rather a problem why he eventually included this study
in the *Appreciations* at all; it is significant only of a
certain catholicity of taste, and bears but few traces of
his own temperament.

But Pater was now hard at work on an interesting
series of experiments of a kind that he may be held to
have originated. These are the *Imaginary Portraits*,
of which the first, "A Prince of Court Painters," was
written in 1885, as soon as *Marius* was off his hands;
two others followed in 1886—"Sebastian van Storck"
and "Denys l'Auxerrois"—and a fourth in 1887, "Duke
Carl of Rosenmold." But beside these four, which com-
pose the volume known as *Imaginary Portraits*, there were
several others which may be referred to the same class.
"The Child in the House," which has been already
treated of, is one. "Hippolytus Veiled," the work of
1889, is another, which has been dealt with among the

Greek Studies, with which he included it.   He told
Mr. Arthur Symons at the end of his life that he
intended to bring out a new volume of *Imaginary
Portraits*. "Apollo in Picardy," the work of 1893, was
to have been included, as well as "Emerald Uthwart"
(1892), of which we have spoken.   He added that
he meant to write one on the picture by Moroni
known as *The Tailor*, which he thought a very fine
and dignified figure.   He would make him, he said,
a Burgomaster.   Mr. Ainslie says that he had in
his mind Count Raymond of Toulouse as another
possible subject.

Pater's method was to take some romantic figure
which attracted his attention, to form a conception of
the temperament of the man, and study his environment as far as possible.   He then would amplify the
details, working in historical hints; or else, as in
the case of "Denys l'Auxerrois," it would be a pure
fantasy, suggested by some trace of a peculiar mind
revealed in the architecture or sculpture of a particular
building.

This was perhaps the most congenial field for a
temperament like Pater's, that was imaginative rather
than creative, that needed a definite *motif* to set his
imagination at work.

Thus in the *Imaginary Portraits* Pater gave himself up
to the luxurious pleasure of evolving fantasies arising
from some biographical hint, some piece of unnamed
art; some type of character that he conceived.   They
are true creations, worked out in a sober pictorial
manner.   But they make it abundantly clear that he
had not the dramatic gift; there is no attempt at de-
vising the play of situations, no contrast of character.
The backgrounds, both of people and of landscape, are
finely indicated; but the interest in each concentrates

upon a single figure, and they are told in a species of
dreamy recitative.

"A Prince of Court Painters" is the story of
Antony Watteau told in the home-keeping journal
of a girl of his own age, daughter of a craftsman of Valenciennes, who perhaps loves him, though
with the reticence so characteristic of the author this
only emerges in a shadowy hint here and there. The
journal is extraordinarily graceful, and exhibits, to give
it verisimilitude, many French turns of expression and
phrase, as though it had been originally conceived in
French; but the whole lacks vital truth; there is too
much philosophy of a hinted kind, too much criticism;
the omission, for instance, of a dozen deliberate phrases
indicating the supposed sex of the writer, might convert the whole into the work of a pensive man. There
is little sentiment or emotion, though it is faintly
illuminated as by a setting sun with a tender aloofness,
a spectacular dreamfulness—a beautiful quality and
finely conceived, but yet with little hold on nature.

There is a characteristic thread of personal interest
interwoven with the story. The girl who writes the
journal is the sister of Jean Baptiste Pater, the pupil
of Watteau; and the artistic progress of her brother,
his enthusiastic admiration for his master, his patient
development, which is sharply contrasted with the
fitful and restless energy of Watteau, plays a real
though a secondary part in the study. It is also
highly characteristic of Pater's reticent delicacy that,
though he liked to fancy the painter a collateral member of his own family, the actual name of Pater is
never introduced into the piece, the brother figuring
throughout simply as Jean Baptiste.

But there is an abundance of fine criticism both of
life and art in the whole picture. Could the charm

of Watteau be more delicately captured than in the
following passage ?—

> "And at last one has actual sight of his work—what it is.
> He has brought with him certain long-cherished designs to
> finish here in quiet, as he protests he has never finished
> before. That charming *Noblesse*—can it be really so distin-
> guished to the minutest point, so naturally aristocratic ?
> Half in masquerade, playing the drawing-room or garden
> comedy of life, these persons have upon them, not less than
> the landscape he composes, and among the accidents of which
> they group themselves with such a perfect fittingness, a cer-
> tain light we should seek for in vain upon anything real. For
> their framework they have around them a veritable archi-
> tecture — a tree-architecture — to which those moss-grown
> balusters, *termes*, statues, fountains, are really but accessories.
> Only, as I gaze upon those windless afternoons, I find myself
> always saying to myself involuntarily, 'The evening will be
> a wet one.' The storm is always brooding through the massy
> splendour of the trees, above those sun-dried glades or lawns,
> where delicate children may be trusted thinly clad ; and
> the secular trees themselves will hardly outlast another
> generation."

Throughout the whole of the study, as one might
expect, the personality of Pater emerges in little
dicta and comments. "Alas !" writes the girl, "How
little peace have his great successes given him ; how
little of that quietude of mind, without which, me-
thinks, one fails in true dignity of character."

The interest, then, of this little study lies not so
much in itself, as in the fact that it is from the
creative point of view the most ambitious, the most
deliberately dramatic, of Pater's writings. He attempted to throw himself into a French mood, and
in this he has partially succeeded ; and into the mood
of a quiet girl of the bourgeois class ; and here he
must be held to have failed. Perhaps it revealed to

him his own limitations, his own strength. For he wisely wrote no more in this manner.

In "Denys l'Auxerrois" we have one of the most fantastic of all Pater's writings; indeed, in this strange combination of the horrible and the beautiful, there is something almost unbalanced, something that reminds one of the rich madness of Blake; as if the mind, though kept in artistic check, had flung itself riotously over the line that divides imagination from insanity; the fancy seems to struggle and trample with a strange self-born fury, as though it had taken the bit in its teeth, and was with difficulty overmastered. The essay begins soberly enough with a vein of quiet reminiscence of travel; the writer is supposed to see some tapestries at a priest's house representing a series of strange experiences; and it is upon this that the story is based. Denys of Auxerre, a love-child, comes among the craftsmen of the place, like a pagan god incarnate, and fills them, like Dionysus, with a species of Bacchic fury. This idea, the reappearance of pagan deities, had a strong fascination for Pater's mind.

The curious and contradictory traits of the character of the boy, gentleness side by side with cruelty, wild courage shadowed by unreasonable terrors, his unaccountable appearances and disappearances, his mysterious gifts of presage and inspiration, are all subtly indicated.

"Long before it came he could detect the scent of rain from afar, and would climb with delight to the great scaffolding on the unfinished tower to watch its coming over the thirsty vine-land, till it rattled on the great tiled roof of the church below; and then, throwing off his mantle, allow it to bathe his limbs freely, clinging firmly against the tempestuous wind among the carved imageries of dark stone."

A climax of horror is reached when a search is made for the buried body of a patron saint of the church, till, in the uncertain light of morning, the coffin is found and opened, and the bishop with his gloved hands draws out the shrouded shrunken form. At this Denys has an access of terror, and rolls in a fit upon the grass. But he recovers himself, and though by this time suspected of sorcery, he gives much anxious care to the setting up of the great organ of the church.

"The carpenters, under his instruction, set up the great wooden passages for the thunder; while the little pipes of pasteboard simulated the sound of the human voice singing to the victorious notes of the long metal trumpets."

At last he ventures to appear in public at a pageant. The haircloth he wears scratches his lips and makes them bleed, and at the sight, an unholy fury fills the crowd. He is literally torn in pieces.

"The soul of Denys was already at rest, as his body, now borne along in front of the crowd, was tossed hither and thither, torn at last limb from limb. The men stuck little shreds of his flesh, or, failing that, of his torn raiment, into their caps; the women lending their long hairpins for the purpose."

In such a passage as this the horror passes beyond the range of perfect art; and the shadow is heightened by the natural tranquillity and austerity of the writer. One cannot help feeling that Pater was here over-powered by his conception, and that he allowed to escape him, for almost the only time in his writings, a kind of almost animal zest in blood and carnage. There is no lack of what is commonly called power, but there is a lack of the restraint which as a rule

Pater so diligently preached. It reminds one of the
tale of Tod Lapraik in *Catriona*, where the staid and
smiling weaver dances alone in a hollow of the rocks
in the black glory of his heart; or of the still more
grim story of Kipling, where the veil that separates
the man from the brute is twitched aside, and the unhappy wretch, intoxicated by a bestial instinct, asks
eagerly for raw meat, and rolls and digs in the earth
beneath the dark shrubs of the garden.

'Sebastian van Storck" is an astonishing contrast
to the last. The *motif* of the essay is devotion to the
purest and most abstract reason. Sebastian is a young
Hollander, the son of a Burgomaster of wealth and
high social position. The young Sebastian, a graceful
finished nature, but with a strain of phthisis in his
constitution, is a lonely, isolated young man, out of
sympathy with the rich, phlegmatic, easy life which
surrounds him, who is drawn into a track of abstract
intellectual speculation, partly by a certain mortal
coldness of temperament, and partly by a clear and
logical faculty of thought. He becomes interested in
the philosophy of the young Spinoza, who is a friend
and contemporary, and he sets out upon a chilly
pilgrimage of thought with a kind of intellectual dis-
interestedness, till he arrives at the conclusion that
the only use to make of life is to cultivate a severe
detachment from all its interests and ties. His view
of God becomes ever colder and more impersonal.

" For him, that one abstract being was as the pallid Arctic
sun, disclosing itself over the dead level of a glacial, a barren
and absolutely lonely sea. The lively purpose of life had
been frozen out of it. What he must admire, and love if he
could, was ' equilibrium,' the void, the *tabula rasa*, into which,
through all those apparent energies of man and nature, that
in truth are but forces of disintegration, the world was really

settling. And, himself a mere circumstance in a fatalistic series, to which the clay of the potter was no sufficient parallel, he could not expect to be 'loved in return.' "

The crisis comes by his being almost drawn into a marriage with a beautiful girl of his own circle. He has to a certain extent submitted to her charm, and the betrothal is looked upon as an event daily to be expected. The girl herself falls under the spell of Sebastian's beauty and fascination; and at a social gathering at which the friends of both expect and desire the pledge to be given and accepted, she betrays a certain innocent coquetry, which in Sebastian's tense mood acts like water dashed in his face. He is filled with a sharp disgust and flies from home, taking refuge in a lonely manor-house, the property of his family. A spell of stormy weather succeeds and the land is inundated. When at last it is possible to reach the lonely house through the raging flood Sebastian is found dead, having apparently lost his life in saving a child, who is discovered unhurt wrapped in Sebastian's furs.

Pater seems in this essay to have endeavoured, we will not say to enforce the dangers of the intellectual pursuit of abstraction, for the picture has hardly an ethical motive, but to depict in neutral tints the natural course of the quest of pure reason. It is a melancholy essay. Sebastian seems to suffocate under warmth and light; and the whole sketch has something of the frozen silence, the mute impassivity of the stiffened leafless earth. It is more like a piece of cold and colourless sculpture than a picture; and the contrast of the stainless icy figure of the victim of thought thrown into relief by the warm, fire-lit, comfortable indoor world, peopled with types of indolent and contented materialists, is skilfully enough wrought. But the subtle beauty of the treatment does not remove a certain inner dreariness of thought, and the central figure seems to shiver underneath the rich robe draped about it.

"Duke Carl of Rosenmold" is an eighteenth-century study of a very different temperament. He is the heir of an aged Grand-Duke, and is full to the brim of enthusiasm for art, music, literature, and nature. But just as Sebastian van Storck was the victim of an excess of intellectual power, so Duke Carl is the victim of its defect. His soul is in revolt against stolid German heaviness; he is a typical figure of the spirit of the Renaissance, all athirst for beauty and novelty. But his temperament is whimsical and unbalanced; he has little originality or lucidity of thought; he falls under the spell of all that is rococo, and mistakes novelty for energy; he takes up each new interest with eager zest, but too soon tires of it; to relieve the dreariness of satiety in the search for new sensations, he causes his death to be announced and is present in disguise at his own funeral. Here he parts company with soundness of mind, and in his rebellion against all that is conventional he mistakes the true stuff out of which unconventionality is made. The true creative genius, to use a metaphor, accepts the conventions of the age as a sort of necessary frame to impulse, and troubles his head little about it; his concern is with the picture itself, how to make it perfectly sincere, perfectly impressive. But Duke Carl's originality is vitiated by the desire to startle and surprise timid natures, and to have his originality admired or at least recognised. His grandfather abdicates, and soon after dies, and Duke Carl's mind, which has been distracted for a while by foreign travel, becomes set upon marriage with a peasant girl, partly from real affection, partly from a desire to do the unexpected thing. His end is somewhat mysterious; he arranges to meet his betrothed in a lonely stronghold, and falls a victim to an armed invasion. Contrary to his habit, instead of letting the story speak for itself, Pater appends a conclusion in which he says that his object has been to sketch a precursor of what may be called the German Renaissance, of Lessing and Herder, leading on to Goethe. But the interest remains psychical rather than historical. The duke is a type of those natures who, with an intense susceptibility to artistic influences, have no real force of character or conception in the background, and fall victims to a neurotic desire, which approaches near to vulgarity, to cause a commotion among stolid and commonplace persons, because they are conscious of their inability, from want of real intellectual energy, to impress or influence the higher natures.

The whole volume, then, is based on an idea of intellectual and artistic revolt; each of the four types depicted, Watteau, Denys, Sebastian, and Duke Carl, is a creature born out of due time, and suffering from the isolation that necessarily comes from the consciousness of being out of sympathy with one's environment. In all four there is a vein of physical malady. Watteau and Sebastian are phthisical, and Denys and Duke Carl are of unbalanced mind. This tendency to dwell on what is diseased and abnormal has a curious psychological interest; and it will be observed, too, that all the four figures depicted are youthful heroes, endowed with charm and beauty, but all overshadowed by a presage of death. There is thus something of the *macabre*, the decadent element about the book.

It will be as well here to consider the two other Imaginary Portraits, "Emerald Uthwart" (1892) and

"Apollo in Picardy" (1893), because, though of slightly later date, they in reality belong to the same series.

"Apollo in Picardy" is one of the purest pieces of fantasy that Pater ever composed. In its *motif* it much resembles "Denys l'Auxerrois," the conception being that of a reincarnation of a sort of pagan spirit, perhaps a fallen deity, in the midst of a monastic world.

Prior Saint-Jean, bred as a monk, is occupied in middle age in the composition of an abstruse book of astronomy and music, dry and scientific enough. He is sent, being in indifferent health, down to the Grange of the monastery, to superintend the building of a great monastic barn. He takes with him a novice named Hyacinth, the pet of the community, neat, serviceable, frank, boyish. The first evening after their arrival the Prior goes into the granary, and finds there asleep among the fleeces a young serf of the monastery, a youth of extraordinary beauty, with a strange harp lying beside him. The Prior mutters a collect, conscious of a certain unholy charm, and goes softly away. The next day he finds the serf waiting upon them. The great barn is built, and a series of mysterious and inexplicable circumstances occurs. The serf seems to inspire a sort of wild gaiety, a spontaneous art into the builders, and manifests, too, an almost Satanical strength.

The boy Hyacinth finds this strange creature a delightful playmate; and yet there is a bewildering mixture of charm and cruelty about him. The wild creatures of the forest will come at his call; he will play with them, and when tired of play will pierce them with an arrow or snap their fragile backs. Yet they nestle to him to die in his arms.

Sometimes the cruelty breaks out in horrible ways. One evening the great pigeon-house is invaded by some creature unknown, which destroys the birds wholesale, leaving their bodies ruthlessly rent and torn. Yet next day the serf comes weeping to the mass; the chapel is found to be strangly decked with exotic flowers, and the serf himself joins with his harp in the canticles, drawing the rough voices to a silvery music.

The Prior feels the magical influences of the place slowly involving him. He turns to his book, but there seems a madness in his brain. Instead of penning dry scientific discussions, he finds himself impelled against his will to crowd strange drawings and illuminations into his book, "winged flowers, or stars with human limbs and faces, still intruding themselves, or mere notes of light and darkness from the actual horizon."

He comes to again and again from his wild work with a shock of terror and disgust. The boy Hyacinth becomes terrified at the Prior's strange illusions, his loss of memory, his feverish periods of what seems such unhallowed work. But one hot, breathless evening he is drawn to play again with the serf, whom he begins to mistrust. They play with an ancient quoit, which is turned up from a grave. Stript to the skin in wild excitement, they play late into the night, till the quoit flung by the serf, whether by accident or a sudden bloody impulse none knows, crashes into the boy's brain, and leaves him dead on the turf.

The serf flies ; the Prior falls under suspicion of the murder ; but is claimed by the monastic authorities and confined as obviously insane. He spends long hours gazing out of the windows, weeping, uttering strange words ; till at last his senses return to him, but he dies just as his release is permitted.

The study is full of beauty from end to end, beauty
and strangeness side by side. Yet it is hard not to
feel a sort of distempered, almost riotous, fancy at work
under it all, and there is a cloistered horror about it,
that reminds one of the old monastic legend of the
monk who goes late into the dark church to recover
a volume that he had left there, and finds a strange
merry thing, in the habit of a priest, leaping all alone
in unholy mirth before the altar.

It may be said that this is exactly the effect which
the writer intended to produce, and the art is manifest.
But for all that there is a species of uncanny terror
which invests the tale; not the terror which may involve the narrative of one who has seen strange things
and records them faithfully, but the terror with which
one might watch a magician trafficking in breathless
secrets, with a certain dark power of using energies
which seem to menace alike serenity and virtue.

"Emerald Uthwart" is a little fantasy written in
1892. The incidents related are simple enough, and yet
in a way sensational. Emerald is the son of an ancient
English family, brought up in an old Sussex home, long
the property of his ancestors, people of an unemphatic
type. "Why! the Uthwarts had scarcely had more
memories than their woods, noiselessly deciduous."
He goes to school, contrary to the tradition of the
family, and the scene of his education is laid at what is
obviously the King's School, Canterbury. Here he
forms a great friendship with a boy a little older than
himself, James Stokes; they go on to Oxford together,
get commissions in the army, in consequence of the
breaking out afresh of a war, the scene of which is
laid in Flanders. They are kept waiting before a
beleaguered town; James Stokes conceives a plan of
entering the town with a few men on an expedition

the object of which is obscure. They enter the town, secure their prize—a weather-beaten flag—and issue out again to find that the army has moved on; they rejoin their regiment, are tried by court-martial, and condemned to death. They are led out to execution, and when James Stokes has been shot, the scene being described with a grim realism, it is announced that Emerald's sentence has been commuted into one of degradation and dismissal. This is carried out; he wanders about in want and wretchedness, but finally makes his way home, where he eventually dies, after a lingering illness of four years, from an old wound, aggravated by hardship and mental suffering. Just before the end his case is brought before the military authorities, and he receives an offer of a commission. The story ends by a somewhat terrible extract supposed to be from a surgeon's diary, who removes the ball from the wound.

The *motif* of the story is to depict a certain type of Englishman, a type of decorous submissiveness. But the interest of the type lies rather in the attempt that is made to represent it in a character of great modesty and simplicity, but with a high natural charm both of manner and physical appearance.

The weakness of the conception may be said to lie in the fact, that apart from this external and physical charm the character is rather essentially uninteresting — unambitious and demure — a Spartan, not an Athenian type.

It was probably Pater's object to depict the Spartan element of public-school education; and it is here that the main interest of the sketch lies.

"In fact," he says, "by one of our wise English compromises, we still teach our so modern boys the Classics; a lesson in attention and patience, at the least. Nay! by a double compromise, with delightful physiognomic results sometimes, we teach them their pagan Latin and Greek under the shadow of medieval church-towers, amid the haunts, the traditions, and with something of the discipline, of monasticism ; for which, as is noticeable, the English have never wholly lost an early inclination. . . . The result of our older method has had its value so far, at least, say ! for the careful aesthetic observer. It is of such diagonal influences, through complication of influence, that expression comes, in life, in our culture, in the very faces of men and boys—of these boys. Nothing could better harmonise present with past than the sight of them just here, as they shout at their games, or recite their lessons, over-arched by the work of medieval priors, or pass to church meekly, into the seats occupied by the young monks before them."

But there is a certain want of naturalness about the conception. The picture of James Stokes descanting to his friend on minute points of meaning in Homer, in Virgil, lacks reality. Emerald himself, after being punished by the head-master, stands up and says, " And now, sir, that I have taken my punishment, I hope you will forgive my fault." Not so do English boys behave ! And it is just here, in these rare touches of attempted drama, that Pater's art invariably breaks down. He was aware that his own instinct was not dramatic. He wrote (August 9, 1891) to a friend, Mr. Douglas Ainslie, thanking him for a copy of a play which Mr. Ainslie had published, saying that he would read it with interest, but adding "the dramatic form of literature is not what I usually turn to with most readiness."

Submissiveness, he says, was the key of Uthwart's character : "it had the force of genius with him " ; he entered into his work with serious obedience, but feeling that the perception of great literature was something unattainable by himself ; religion too, "its high claims, to which no one could be equal ; its reproaches "

—he felt it all to be immeasurable, "surely not meant for the like of him." He is always "repressible, self-restrained, always concurring with the influence, the claim upon him, the rebuke, of others." He attracts the notice of strangers by his unconscious grace and healthy beauty ; he is surprised at the charm he exerts on others, never elated by it, nor presuming upon it. And no doubt it is the intention of the piece to show how his one violation of duty, his single deviation from strict military obedience, brought with it ruin and death—so apparently disproportionate a punishment. But he takes his degradation with the same humble submissiveness, and it is in the same spirit that he meets his death, not repining nor complaining, but simply as the orders of some superior power, whom he is to obey unflinchingly by a sort of sacred instinct. The purpose of the piece, then, is to draw out the beauty of the obedient character, a soldierlike simplicity and tranquillity. It is hardly necessary to add that the accessories are exquisitely finished ; the old house, with its scented flower-beds and venerable chambers; the ancient stately school, with the Cathedral to which it is attached ; but in this one essay it may be said that the simplicity of the motive does not wholly harmonise with the delicacy of the setting. The thought is tinged and coloured by being seen through a somewhat self-conscious and sensuous medium. One cannot help feeling that Emerald would have disliked being regarded in this light, being made a picture of; that is perhaps no reason why it should not be attempted, but it militates against the success of the story, because one feels that Emerald is caught like a butterfly, in the gauzy meshes of a net, and is being too intimately, too tenderly, scrutinised, when he is made for the free air and the sun.

And, artistically speaking, one cannot help regarding the extract with which the story ends as a blot. The operation for the removal of the ball, the replacing of the body in the coffin, with "the peak of the handsome nose remaining visible among the flowers"—one feels this to be a harsh realism, with an almost morbid dwelling upon the accidents of mortality, which does a certain violence to the whole conception. Thus, though there are passages in "Emerald Uthwart" which must always rank high among the achievements of Pater, it is impossible to resist the feeling that in this painful story he was attempting effects to which his art could not rise.

It is not, I think, fanciful to interpret this selection of types in the light of Pater's own life, the half-lit atmosphere in which he deliberately or perhaps temperamentally moved. They are the work of a melancholy introspective mind, dwelling wistfully upon the outer beauty of the world, but with a deeper current of mournful amazement at the brevity and the mystery of it all. No doubt Pater, too, felt his own isolation heavily rather than acutely. Did he belong, one can imagine his asking himself, in spirit, to the earlier, more fragrant, more insouciant time, when men were less shadowed by the complexity of thought and the inherited conscience of the ages? Or did he belong to some future outburst of simpler, more liberal joy, to a time when the heavy commercialism of England, its conventional politics, its moral confusion, its mercantile view of education should be leavened by beauty and sincere joy? Whichever it was, he had fallen on evil days. Oxford itself, that should have been the home of intellectual and artistic speculation, was crowded by a younger generation, whose idea of a University was a place where, among social and athletic delights, it was

possible to defer for a time the necessity of adopting
practical life. The older men, those who were accepted by the academical world as men of leading, were
too often men of bursarial minds, who loved business
and organisation better than intellectual freedom.
Even the keener spirits, both among the younger and
the older men, were of the dry and rigid type, believ-
ing in accuracy more than ideas, in definite accumulation more than intellectual enjoyment. In this
atmosphere Pater felt himself misunderstood and
decried. The daring and indiscreet impulses of youth
had died away, and his unconventionalism had cost
him dear. What wonder that his thoughts took on a
melancholy tinge, and that he recurred in mind to the
thought of figures whose unlikeness to those about
them, in spite of the fine daring, the beautiful impulses
of their nature, had brought them dissatisfaction and
disaster and even death!

CHAPTER VI

LATER WRITINGS

ALL this time Pater was engaged upon a great work, which was destined never to be finished. *Gaston de Latour* was embarked upon soon after the completion of *Marius*. Five chapters appeared in *Macmillan's Magazine* in the course of 1888. A sixth chapter appeared in the *Fortnightly Review* in the next year under the title of "Giordano Bruno," and various other unfinished fragments remain. The chapter called "Shadows of Events" is the only one of these which has been included in the 1902 volume. In the case of a writer as sedulous, as eager for perfection as Pater it is right to withhold the incomplete fragments. He seems for some cause to have abandoned the book in dissatisfaction. We may speculate as to the cause of this. I am myself disposed to think that he found the historical setting too complicated and the canvas too much crowded. As the story advances the personality seems to ebb out of the figure of the hero, and he becomes a mere mirror of events and other personalities. The influences, too, that are brought to bear on him are of so complicated a nature that his development seems hampered rather than enlarged. No doubt Pater felt that the book was not exhibiting his own best qualities of workmanship; and there is a growing weariness visible, as if he felt that he was failing to cope with the pressure of historical experience that was closing in upon the central figure.

It may here be said that Pater's best work is that which is built up delicately and imaginatively out of shadowy hints of events and slender records. His power lay in filling in, heightening, and enriching faint outlines, not in selecting typical touches from great masses of detail. He felt, and rightly, that he had mistaken his capacity. The period he had chosen, the struggle of Huguenots and Catholics, is crowded with salient figures, but to treat it romantically, the tact, the swift intuition of such a writer as Walter Scott was needed, sketching in broad washes and bold strokes; not the patient and accumulative toil of a minute and delicate writer like Pater.

The story opens beautifully enough. The boy Gaston lives the quiet life of the country at the old house of Deux-manoirs in La Beauce, the central corn-land of France, with the dim shape of the great church of Chartres visible, like a ship under press of canvas, on the low horizon.

Gaston is of the same type as Marius—innocent, serious, devout, keenly sensitive to impressions of beauty. We see him first taking upon himself the vows of the ecclesiastical life, "duly arrayed for dedication, with the lighted candle in his right hand and the surplice folded over his left shoulder," in the dark glowing church.

Somehow the figure fails to appeal to us. We feel—could Pater have felt the same?—that we are but meeting Marius over again in altered circumstances.

Yet the description of the Office, sung in the presence of the courtly and vivacious Bishop of Chartres, is full of beauty :—

"It was like a stream of water crossing unexpectedly a dusty way—*Mirabilia testimonia tua!* In psalm and antiphon, inexhaustibly fresh, the soul seemed to be taking refuge, at that undevout hour, from the sordid languor and the mean business of men's lives, in contemplation of the unfaltering vigour of the divine righteousness, which had still those who sought it, not only watchful in the night but alert in the drowsy afternoon. Yes! there was the sheep astray, *sicut ovis quae periit*—the physical world ; with its lusty ministers, at work, or sleeping for a while amid the stubble, their faces upturned to the August sun—the world so importunately visible, intruding a little way, with its floating odours, in that semicircle of heat across the old over-written pavement at the great open door, upon the mysteries within."

The quiet life of the Manor is broken shortly afterwards by a sudden visit of the young King Charles the Ninth, who enters from a hunting expedition, and "with a relish for the pleasant cleanliness of the place" utters a shrill strain of half-religious oaths. Pale, with an ivory whiteness, vivacious, unbalanced, the young king feels the charm of the place, touches a lute, talks of verses, and scratches a stanza of his own with a diamond upon a window-pane.

As Gaston lives on his quiet life in a disturbed and alarmed country his reflective nature begins to open. "In the sudden tremor of an aged voice, the handling of a forgotten toy, a childish drawing, in the tacit observance of a day, he became aware suddenly of the great stream of human tears falling always through the shadows of the world."

He goes on to join the episcopal household of Chartres as a page, in the company of other noble youths. He makes friends ; books and talk—"the brilliant surface of the untried world "—confront him ; but his own calm instinct, his tranquillising sense of religion, provide the necessary balance. He takes three

chosen companions home with him to spend the hot
bright weeks of the summer; and here, through the
poems of Ronsard, the infection of the living and
breathing spirit of the modern poetry, near, actual,
tangible like the faces of flowers, seizes upon him.

"Never before had words, single words, meant so much.
What expansion, what liberty of heart, in speech : how associ-
able to music, to singing, the written lines ! He sang of the
lark, and it was the lark's voluble self. The physical beauty
of humanity lent itself to every object, animate or inanimate,
to the very hours and lapses and changes of time itself.
An almost burdensome fulness of expression haunted the
gestures, the very dress, the personal ornaments, of the people
on the highway." "Here, was a discovery, a new faculty, a
privileged apprehension, to be conveyed in turn to one and to
another, to be propagated for the imaginative regeneration of
the world."

In this excited mood he rides with his companions
to the Priory, not far away, of which Ronsard was the
Prior, to see the great man himself. And here Pater
is at his best. They find the Prior himself digging in
his garden; they attend a solemnity in the church;
they sup with the poet, who, touched by the generous
enthusiasm of the boys, abandons himself to a sociable
mood, shows them his treasures, his manuscripts, his
portraits. But Gaston finds that Ronsard has attained
to no serenity of spirit; his "roving, astonished eyes"
reveal him as "the haggard soul of a haggard generation."

Ronsard is sympathetically interested in the ardent
spirit of the boy, and gives him an introduction to the
great Montaigne; whom he presently goes to visit, in
his château in Dordogne.

"It was pleasant to sleep as if in the sea's arms, amid the
low murmurs, the salt odour mingled with the wild garden

scents of a little inn or farm, forlorn in the wide enclosure of an
ancient manor, deserted as the sea encroached—long ago, for
the fig-trees in the riven walls were tough and old."

He finds the great man in his towered manor, with
the view from the roof of the rich noonday scenery.
He feels after a few moments' talk as if he had known
the genial philosopher all his life.

"In the presence of this indefatigable analyst of act and
motive all fixed outlines seemed to vanish away.   The health-
ful pleasure of motion, of thoughts in motion ! "

"Montaigne was constantly, gratefully, announcing his
contact, in life, in books, with undeniable power and
greatness, with forces full of beauty in their vigour, like
lightning, the sea, the torrents."

The portrait of this splendid human egotist is
admirably touched, with a wealth of subtle illustration
from his writings. His deeply sceptical spirit, his
vivid agnosticism, confronted again and again with
hopeless mysteries, and yet for ever turning back
upon the quest, undaunted, unsated, absolutely sincere,
admitting his own egotism with frank humour—"in
favour of the Huguenots, who condemn our private
confession, I confess myself in public." And this
outward egotism of manner was but the symptom of
a certain deeper doctrinal egotism ;—"I have no other
end in writing but to discover *myself*."

Pater indicates, with perfect insight, the "broad,
easy, indifferent" passage of Montaigne through the
world, his relish for meat and drink and corporeal
sensation ; and yet, side by side with this, a curious,
superstitious, formal kind of piety, all springing from
the same worship for the whole of humanity. But
after all, it was the sincerity and tolerance of the man
that was the charm, his quaint fancy, his rich

sympathy, his perfect comprehension; the influence
that he exercised was that of one who made no selection of moods and things, but tasted all, enjoyed all.

Then follows the chapter called "Shadows of
Events," which it was well to publish, but about which
it is easy to comprehend Pater's own hesitation. It is
a historical survey mainly, but the impression is all
clouded and blurred; one cannot help feeling that the
one thing lacking to Pater was the very largeness
of tolerance which he described so admiringly in
Montaigne; certain characteristics, certain brilliant
points attract him; but he cannot visualise what he
does not admire. The characters that play a large,
robust, coarse, straightforward part are all outside of
him, incomprehensible, repellent. The types whom
Pater discerned so clearly were those who crept somewhat remotely, spectatorially, even timidly through
the throng, who lived the interior life of thought and
speculation and appreciation, tasting the finer savours;
not those who strode out boldly, feeling the air of the
world their native air. Something of this melancholy
aloofness was true of Pater himself, and he draws near
only to those in whom he discerns something of the
same wistful remoteness.

"Looking back afterwards," says Pater of Gaston, "this
singularly self-possessed person had to confess that under
(the) influence (of the unsettled conditions of the age) he had
lost for a while the exacter view of certain outlines, certain
real differences and oppositions of things in that hotly-
coloured world of Paris,—like a shaken tapestry about
him."

The last phrase is exactly true of the chapter—it is
a shaken tapestry, a multitude of blurred heads and
faces, confused gestures, agitated forms.

And so we pass to the dignified banishment of Charles, and the arrival of the new king; when across the story breaks the teaching of Bruno—Pantheism, as it is named, "the vision of all things in God," as the end and aim of all metaphysical speculation.

Bruno, originally a Dominican monk, had conceived the idea of the wholeness of life in a spiritual region.

"Through all his pantheistic flights, from horizon to horizon, it was still the thought of liberty that presented itself, to the infinite relish of this 'prodigal son' of Dominic. God the Spirit had made all things indifferently, with a largeness, a beneficence, impiously belied by any theory of restrictions, distinctions, of absolute limitation. Touch ! see ! listen ! eat freely of all the trees of the garden of Paradise, with the voice of the Lord God literally everywhere !—here was the final counsel of perfection."

What repels Gaston in the teaching of Bruno is the want of artistic distinction and refinement about his theory. The instinct of the artist was just that—to define, disentangle, discern, to distinguish between "the precious and the base, aesthetically; between what was right and wrong in the matter of art."

It is not clear then how the doctrine of Bruno or even of Montaigne was to affect the spirit of Gaston. It is a case of a soul the very breath of whose life was the arriving at canons of some kind, whose most sacred duty appeared to be to select, from the immense mass of experience and material flung so prodigally down in the world, the things that belonged to his peace. The difficulty is to comprehend what was to be the issue. In the theory of Montaigne and Bruno alike, Gaston is brought into contact with types essentially uncritical, and one would suppose that they were intended to have an enlarging effect. But the hint seems rather to be that they were to act in the opposite direction, and to throw Gaston back upon the critical attitude, as the one safeguard in the bewildering world.

One feels as though Pater had here essayed too large a task; that he was, so to speak, preaching to himself the doctrine of robust tolerance, of good-humoured sympathy with a more vivid and generous life; and that he could not to his satisfaction depict the next steps in the development because it was precisely the very type of development of which he had had no personal experience.

Thus the book, from its very incompleteness, has the interest of being again an intimate self-revelation. It stands like a great unfinished canvas by a master of minute, imaginative, suggestive portraiture. Only, one is tempted to wish that he had not given so much thought and energy to so baffling a task—that he had constructed more of those solitary figures which he had, as we know, in his mind, in which his powers would have had their full scope, in which every delicate touch would have told.

After the publication of the five chapters of *Gaston de Latour*, Pater gave himself up to the composition of one of the most interesting of all his productions.

The essay on "Style," which appeared in the *Fortnightly Review* of December 1888, and was prefixed to *Appreciations* in 1889, is one of Pater's most elaborate and finished productions. It is indeed so elaborate, so carefully wrought, it disdains so solemnly the devices that bring lucidity, the way-posts and milestones of the road, that in reading it one is apt to lose the sense of its structure, and not to realise what a simple case he is presenting. Professor Seeley used to enunciate the maxim to those whose essays he was criticising, "Let the bones show!" Well, in Pater's essay the bones do not show; not only does the rounded flesh conceal them, but they are still further disguised into a species of pontifical splendour by a rich and stiff embroidered robe of language.

He begins by dismissing with a great subtlety of illustration the ancient principle that a sharp distinction can be drawn between prose and poetry, showing that it is not true that poetry differs only from prose by the presence of metrical restraint; but that while a severe logical structure must underlie poetry, prose can exhibit high imaginative qualities; and that the real distinction in literature is between the literature that is imaginative, and the literature that attempts merely the transcription of fact. He points out that the moment that argument passes from the mere presentation of a theorem and becomes a personal appeal, that moment is the border-line crossed; and that in the work of the historian the poetical element is to be found in the personal element of selection which is bound to come in, and which may then transform statement into art.

"Just in proportion," he says, "as the writer's aim, consciously or unconsciously, comes to be the transcribing, not of the world, not of mere fact, but of his sense of it, he becomes an artist, his work *fine* art; and good art (as I hope ultimately to show) in proportion to the truth of his presentment of that sense; as in those humbler or plainer functions of literature also, truth—truth to bare fact, there—is the essence of such artistic quality as they may have. Truth! there can be no merit, no craft at all, without that. And further, all beauty is in the long run only *fineness* of truth, or what we call expression, the finer accommodation of speech to that vision within."

He goes on to say that imaginative prose is the special art of the modern world, "an instrument of many stops, meditative, observant, descriptive, eloquent, analytic, plaintive, fervid."

He then passes to the proposition that the art of the craftsman of words must be essentially a scholarly art; that the best writer, "with all the jealousy of a lover of words, will resist a constant tendency on the part of the majority of those who use them to efface the distinctions of language"; but there must be no hint of pedantry; the tact of the great writ   being employed in seeing what new words and usages really enrich language and make it elastic and spontaneous, as well as what additions merely debase it.   And then, too, the word-artist must employ "a self-restraint, a skilful economy of means"; every sentence must have its precise relief, "the logically filled space connected always with the delightful sense of difficulty overcome."   He must employ "honourable artifice" to produce a peculiar atmosphere; and thus the perfect artist will be recognised by what he omits even more than by what he retains.   "For in truth all art does but consist in the removal of surplusage, from the last finish of the gem-engraver blowing away the last particle of invisible dust, back to the earliest divination of the finished work to be, lying somewhere, according to Michelangelo's fancy, in the rough-hewn block of stone."

The one essential thing, then, is "that architectural conception of work, which foresees the end in the beginning and never loses sight of it, and in every part is conscious of all the rest, till the last sentence does but, with undiminished vigour, unfold and justify the first."

"All depends upon the original unity, the vital wholeness and identity, of the initiatory apprehension or view."   It must be composition, and not loose accretion. The literary artist must leave off "not in weariness and because he finds *himself* at an end, but in all the freshness of volition."

He admits that there are instances of great writers who have been no artists, who have written with a kind of unconscious tact; but he maintains that one of the greatest pleasures of really good literature is "in the critical tracing out of that conscious artistic structure."

He sums up this part of the subject by saying that all good literature must be directed both by *mind* and *soul*, the mind giving the logical structure, the soul lending the personal appeal.

He then diverges into an elaborate illustration drawn from the methods of Flaubert, whose theory it was that though there might be a number of ways of expressing a thought, yet that there was one perfect way, if the artist could only find it, one unique word, one appropriate epithet, phrase, sentence, paragraph, which alone could express the vision within; and again he enforces his belief in the "special charm in the signs of discovery, of effort and contention towards a due end."

Truth, then, is the essential quality, truth of conception, truth of expression; and style must be characteristic and expressive of personality, and, though taking its form from the conception, must take its colour from the temperament; and indeed that it should do so, that it should indicate the personal colour, is but another manifestation of sincerity.

Thus it will be seen that whether art is good depends upon the soul of the creator, whether it is great depends upon the mind; and then in memorable words he adds that if art

"be devoted further to the increase of men's happiness, to the redemption of the oppressed, or the enlargement of our sympathies with each other, or to such presentment of new or old truth about ourselves and our relation to the world as may ennoble and fortify us in our sojourn here, or immediately, as with Dante, to the glory of God, it will be also great art ; if, over and above those qualities I summed up as mind and soul —that colour and mystic perfume, and that reasonable structure,—it has something of the soul of humanity in it, and finds its logical, its architectural place, in the great structure of human life."

I have dwelt at length on this essay, because in one sense it is the summary of Pater's artistic creed. It is perhaps the only direct and personal revelation of his theory of his art ; but it will be observed throughout that he is speaking not to the outer circle, not even to the critical reader ; it is not a *concio ad populum*, but a *concio ad clerum*. The audience whom he had in mind were the initiated, the craftsmen ; and the whole oration presupposes a species of mystical apprehension of the work of the artist ; hence comes his insistence on the delight that arises from the sense of difficulties overcome, a delight which only the artist who has striven much and failed often can share. It is therefore a technical discourse ; and dealing with it from this point of view, it must be confessed that in two points it falls short of perfect catholicity and reveals the personal bias. The first of these is the point that has just been indicated, that from the highest art of all, such as the art of Shakespeare and Virgil, Dante and Homer, the sense of effort, of obstacles surmounted, disappears. *Celare artem*, that is the triumph ; that the thing should appear simple, easy, inevitable. For in the pleasure that the artist takes in seeing a difficulty successfully wrestled with and overcome, there creeps in a certain self-consciousness, a species of gratified envy in seeing that, supreme as the process is, the difficulty was there; the absence, indeed, of this sense of effort is what keeps many critical students of art away from the highest masterpieces, and allows them to feel more at their ease in art where the mastery is not so complete. But this is a condition that one desires to remove rather than to emphasise; it is based on weakness and fallibility, rather than on strength and confidence.

And the second point, which is allied closely to this, is that Pater presses too heavily upon laboriousness in art at the expense of ecstatic freedom; because though there are among the greatest artists many instances of those who have attained supremacy by endless and painstaking labour, yet, in the case of the best artists of all, they seem to start at a point to which others may hardly attain, to be more like the inheritors of perfect faculty than the laborious acquirers of it. Writers like Scott and Thackeray, for instance, not to travel far for instances, seem to have achieved, as Scott himself said, their best results by a " hurried frankness " of execution, and to have produced by a kind of instinct what others have to learn to produce by toil and thought.

And thus it is that the essay, in its very incompleteness and partiality of view, has an immense value as an autobiographical document, and helps us, if it is the personality of Pater that we desire to apprehend and penetrate, to draw closer to the real man, in his strength and in his limitations, than any other extant writing; and is indeed a piece of intimate self-revelation.

Moreover, the concluding paragraphs of the essay, the frank confession of his belief, in words which his natural reticence make into what may be carelessly regarded as a piece of tame and conventional rhetoric, in the ultimate mission of art, have an intense and vital significance; the increase of sympathy, the amelioration of suffering, the service of humanity—these, then, were in his deliberate view the ends of art. The very use, in the very crucial passage of the summary, of the vague and trite phrase "the glory of God" as a motive for high art, has a poignant emphasis: it reveals the very depth of the writer's soul. He of all men, at the very crisis of the enunciation of his creed, could never have used such an expression unless it contained for him an essential truth; and this single phrase bears eloquent testimony to the fact that, below the aesthetic doctrine which he enunciated, lay an ethical base of temperament, a moral foundation of duty and obedience to the Creator and Father of men.

In the course of 1889—not a prolific year—"Hippolytus Veiled" appeared in *Macmillan's Magazine*, and "Giordano Bruno," one of the Chapters of *Gaston de Latour*, in the *Fortnightly*. Pater also published the *Appreciations*—rather a made-up volume, one is forced to reflect, the kind of book that is issued in response to the appeal of a publisher. We have already discussed all the contents of the volume, except the Shakespearian studies, three in number, of which "Measure for Measure" had appeared in 1874, "Love's Labours Lost" in 1878. "Shakespeare's English Kings" had not appeared before, and was the only new item in the volume. Two facts are noticeable about the book. The essay on "Æsthetic Poetry," written in 1868, reappeared here, but was omitted in the later edition of 1890; and the study called "Romanticism," written in 1876, reappeared as a Postscript.

The Shakespearian studies do not demand any very close attention. In the little essay on "Love's Labours Lost" he points out that in the play Shake-

speare was dallying with Euphuism. "It is this fop-
pery of delicate language, this fashionable plaything
of his time, with which Shakespeare is occupied in
'Love's Labours Lost.'" But he points out, too, that
in dealing with a past age, one cannot afford to neglect
a study of its playthings : "For what is called fashion
in these matters occupies, in each age, much of the
care of many of the most discerning people, furnishing
them with a kind of mirror of their real inward refinements, and their capacity for selection. Such modes
or fashions are, at their best, an example of the artistic
predominance of form over matter ; of the manner of
the doing of it over the thing done ; and have a beauty
of their own." And this, he concludes, is the chief
value of the play.

In the essay on "Measure for Measure" he shows
that the play is a remodelling of an earlier and rougher
composition ; but he points out that the value and
significance of it is that Shakespeare works out of
it "a morality so characteristic that the play might
well pass for the central expression of his moral judgments." He says that we have in it "a real example
of that sort of writing which is sometimes described as
suggestive, and which, by the help of certain subtly
calculated hints only, brings into distinct shape the
reader's own half-developed imaginings." He notes the
dark invasion of the shadow of death in the play,
death the "'great disguiser,' blanching the features of
youth and spoiling its goodly hair, touching the fine
Claudio even with its disgraceful associations." And
further, he touches with exquisite skill the way in
which Shakespeare here brings out, by a sudden
vignette, a romantic picture of a scene ; the episode
of Mariana, "the moated grange, with its dejected
mistress, its long, listless, discontented days, where we

hear only the voice of a boy broken off suddenly in
the midst of one of the loveliest songs of Shakespeare,
or of Shakespeare's school, is the pleasantest of many
glimpses we get here of pleasant places." Not less
delicate is the apprehension of the character of Isabella,
so tranquil, chaste, and sisterly at first, changed, by
the inrush of contending passions, in a moment, into
something fierce, vindictive, and tiger-like. He sums
up his conclusion by saying that the charm of the
work is its underlying conception of morality, not the
morality which opposes a blunt and stubborn front to
the delicate activities of life, but the artistic morality
that watches, judges, values and appreciates, and is on
the side of culture rather than on the side of prejudice
and rectitude.

The essay on "Shakespeare's English Kings" (1889)
is rather a slight performance, and the analysis of a
somewhat superficial kind. Pater, for instance, almost
fails to realise the magnificence of the conception of
Richard II., the tragedy of which consists in the fact
that, at a sudden crisis, a prompt force and vigour are
demanded of a ruler whose nature is full indeed of
wise and fruitful thoughts, but whose position calls for
a bluff and cheerful energy, when all that he can give
is a subtle and contemplative philosophy. But he
traces the general motive finely :—

"No !" he says, "Shakespeare's kings are not, nor are
meant to be, great men : rather, little or quite ordinary
humanity, thrust upon greatness, with those pathetic results,
the natural self-pity of the weak heightened in them into
irresistible appeal to others as the net result of their royal
prerogative. One after another, they seem to lie composed in
Shakespeare's embalming pages, with just that touch of nature
about them, making the whole world akin."

He ends by a subtle passage, not fully worked out,

indicating that as unity of impression in a work of art is its perfect virtue, and as lyrical poetry is the best vehicle for such unity, then "a play attains artistic perfection just in proportion as it approaches that unity of lyrical effect, as if a song or ballad were still lying at the root of it."

In these Shakespearian studies, produced at points so far apart in Pater's life, the chief interest is that he should have approached Shakespeare at all. It is after all another testimony to the width and largeness of Shakespeare's mind, that it should have forced an expression of admiration from a spirit so introspective, so definite in its range, so preoccupied with a theory as Pater's. Moreover, as we have seen, dramatic art had little attraction for him. One feels that he does not enter into the humanity, the profundity, of Shakespeare. He is like a man who hovers about the thickets that lie on the verge of a great forest, peeping into the glades, noting the bright flowers and the sweet notes of hidden birds, but with little desire to thread the wood or penetrate its haunted green heart.

The years 1890 and 1891 were not apparently very fruitful; indeed the latter was one of the six, out of the twenty-nine years of Pater's literary life, in which he published nothing but a review or two; but he was hard at work on his *Plato and Platonism*, which began to appear in 1892.

"Prosper Mérimée" was written as a lecture in 1890, and thus belongs to the last period of Pater's work. He begins by a melancholy summary of the century— Mérimée was born in 1803—a century of disillusionment, in which the ancient landmarks had been removed, and men began to ask themselves whether of all the ancient fabric of tradition, of thought, of prin-

ciples, there was anything certain at all. To make the
best of a changed world—that was the problem; and
thus art and literature would tend to become pastimes,
fierce games born of a desperate sort of make-believe,
just to pass the time that remained. Whatever else
was uncertain, it was at least certain that life had
somehow to be lived; if the great old words like
patriotism, virtue, honour were mere high-sounding
names, and stood only for burnt-out illusions, at least
there was a space to be filled, before the dark hours
came bringing with them the ultimate certainty.

Prosper Mérimée, in Pater's view, is the summary
and type of these tendencies. The world is utterly
hollow to him; his cynicism is complete and all-embrac-
ing. He is indifferent to ideas, to politics, to art; but
there still remains the vast and inconsequent spectacle
of human life to study, to amuse oneself with, to depict with a contemptuous grace. History, artistically
selected and displayed, is perhaps the best distraction
of all. History reveals, no doubt, little but desperate
and passionate illusions, but even so there is a narcotic
interest about the spectacle. Into this quarry of
ancient materials Mérimée flings himself with the zest
and appetite of an energetic mind. And so, too, there
were similar possibilities of romance in the modern
world. Corsica, where the scene of *Colomba* is laid, was
a place still full of primal, simple, passionate emotions—
exaggerated, no doubt, and unreasonable, but still unquestionably there. Even that morbid personal pride
with its passion for revenge, its view of life as a sacrifice to honour, offers a stimulus to the imagination,
though the terror of it is free from all interfusion of
pity.

Pater skilfully indicates the perfect art of Mérimée,
the minute proportion, the horror of all loose and

otiose statement, issuing in a style of which every part is closely tied with every other part, and the end synchronises sharply with the conclusion of the story; and further, he characterises the human charm of the *Lettres à une Inconnue*, where the author seems surprised and baffled by the unsuspected violence of his own emotion; the fine intellectual companionship of which he is in search betraying him suddenly, like a crust of ashes over a smouldering fire.

He concludes with an interesting passage which shows that *impersonality* was the aim of Mérimée's art, so that his books stand "as detached from him as from each other, with no more filial likeness to their maker than if they were the work of another person." The same is true of his style—"the perfection of nobody's style," as Pater cleverly calls it—"fastidiously in the fashion—an expert in all the little, half-contemptuous elegances of which it is capable . . . a nice observer of all that is most conventional."

And thus we see that the absence of soul, of subjectivity, of peculiarities, is at once the weakness and the strength of Mérimée's work. It is all pure mind, and produces a singular harshness of ideal, so that "there are masters of French prose whose art has begun where the art of Mérimée leaves off."

It is a fine piece of critical analysis, perhaps a little overstated, but essentially true. Mérimée does not succeed quite to the extent that Pater thinks in absolute self-effacement, but he has seen clearly enough the spirit of the man; and though his exposition marches somewhat relentlessly on, discarding such evidence as may tell against his theory, yet he has somehow penetrated the secret of this brilliant writer with his flawless polish, his inner hardness, as only a great critic can.

Of the delivery of this lecture on Mérimée, the
President of Magdalen says :—

"A large audience, too large for the ugly and inconvenient
Lecture Room at the Taylorian, came to hear him.   He
seemed surprised and overwhelmed.   I don't think he knew
how much of a celebrity he was, and he seemed a little
frightened.   He read his lecture in a low monotonous voice."

In the same year appeared the " Art Notes in North
Italy."   It is what it professes to be, a little study of
certain Italian painters, jottings from an artistic traveller's diary, and deserves no special consideration,
excepting in so far as it reveals Pater's preferences
and his method.

In 1892, besides the first chapters of *Plato and
Platonism*, and an ingenious and beautiful essay on
the study of Dante, written as an introduction to
Mr. C. L. Shadwell's translation of the *Purgatory*, Pater
published, in successive numbers of the *New Review*,
" Emerald Uthwart," which has been considered among
the *Imaginary Portraits*.   In the same year the essay
on "Raphael" was written, as a lecture, and it thus
differs in style to a certain extent from the more
deliberate literary works, though less, perhaps, in the
case of Pater than would be the case with many
writers.   But he certainly aimed at producing something which should be capable of being apprehended
by an interested listener on a first hearing ; there
is less concentration, less ornament, less economy
of effect than in the more deliberate writings.   The
essay presupposes a certain knowledge of the subject,
and aims at bringing out the central *motif* of the life of
the great painter relieved against a somewhat shadowy
and allusive background of events.   But the central
thought is not lacking in clearness.

"By his immense productiveness, by the even perfection of what he produced, its fitness to its own day,
its hold on posterity, in the suavity of his life, some
would add in the 'opportunity' of his early death,
Raphael may seem a signal instance of the luckiness,
of the good fortune, of genius." This is an admirable
summary; and he adds that upon a careful examination of his works "we shall find even his seemingly
mechanical good fortune hardly distinguishable from
his own patient disposal of the means at hand." He
goes on to show that the supreme charm of Raphael's
nature was in his teachableness, his prompt assimila-
tion of influences, his essential humility and tranquillity; that his genius was not a vivid, tortured
thing, like a lightning-flash, with prodigious efforts
long matured in the womb of the cloud, with intervals
of despairing silence and ineffectiveness—but a tranquil,
equable progress: "genius by accumulation; the transformation of meek scholarship into genius." Pater
says, indeed, that Raphael may be held to be the supreme
example of the truth of the beatitude that the meek
shall inherit the earth. He traces the steps of this
progress. He shows him stainless, unruffled, untainted
by the restlessness of the age that flowered in sin, and
yet able by a supreme insight to transfer the hinted
presence of fantastic evil into his pictures; he shows
his gradual mastery of dramatic intensity, till he could
concentrate the whole of a picture on one point, subordinate the whole scene to some central and poignant
emotion. And he brings out, too, with great skill,
that Raphael was always in his own thought a learner,
with no desperate prejudice for originality, always
open to influence, yet transfiguring and transmuting
influence into higher and higher conceptions of his
own. At last he brings him to Rome, where his life

seems "as we read of it, hasty and perplexed, full
of undertakings, of vast works not always to be completed, of almost impossible demands on his industry,
in a world of breathless competition, amid a great
company of spectators, for great rewards." Among
these mighty tasks stands foremost his divergence
into architecture, appointed, as he was, to succeed
Bramante as architect of St. Peter's. But all through
shines out the unspoilt nature, making its charm felt
upon artists and courtiers alike, the same unhasting,
unresting diligence, the same smiling youthfulness of
demeanour.

He shows the mental force of Raphael's conceptions,
his unequalled power of apprehending and transmit-
ting to others complex and difficult ideas with a real
philosophical grasp, yet for all his technique, all his
wealth of antiquarian knowledge, never losing sight
of essential beauty and peace. Pater instances as the
supremely salient instance of his art the Ansidei or
Blenheim Madonna now in the National Gallery. It
is not impossible that he was guided in this selection
by a consideration for those whose opportunities for
acquainting themselves with Raphael's art were bound
to be limited. "I find there," he says, "at first sight,
with something of the pleasure one has in a proposition
of Euclid, a sense of the power of the understanding,
in the economy with which he has reduced his material
to the simplest terms, has disentangled and detached
its various elements." "Keep then to that picture,"
he adds, "as the embodied formula of Raphael's
genius." The conclusion of the essay comes rather
suddenly, and he sums up the purpose of Raphael's
life in the phrase, "I am utterly purposed that I will
not offend." It is this balance of temperament, this
steady deliberate bias to perfect purity, that is the note

of his life.   He is the Galahad of art, and might say
with Galahad—

> " My strength is as the strength of ten,
>   Because my heart is pure."

The essay is thus a careful and sympathetic attempt
to give to learners a lucid introduction to the art of
Raphael.   But it differs from his own chosen subjects,
and is therefore less characteristic of Pater as a writer
than much of his work—in that there is no attempt at
tracing the recondite, the suggestive element in the
work of Raphael.   He intermingles little of his own
preference, his own personality with the verdict; but
it is still deeply characteristic of Pater in another
region of his mind, of the patient sympathy which he
was always ready to give, of his desire to meet others
halfway, not to mystify or to bewilder the half-culti-
vated learner, whose zeal perhaps may outrun his
critical knowledge, with more remote considerations,
but to draw the rays into a single bright focus, rather
than, as Pater so often did, resolve the single ray into
rainbow tints and prismatic refractions.   Here, then,
at least, we see Pater in the light of the educator, the
scribe, the expounder of mysteries, rather than as the
hieratic presenter of the deeper symbol.

Plato and Platonism, certain chapters of which appeared in 1892, was eventually published in 1893, and
thus was the main and serious occupation of Pater's
last years.   He placed the book at the head of his
own writings.   A friend once asked him whether he
thought that *The Renaissance* or *Marius* was his best
book.   "Oh, no," he said, "neither.   If there is anything of mine that has a chance of surviving, I should
say it was my *Plato*."

I do not propose here to discuss the accuracy and the

justice of his picture of the Platonic philosophy, or how far it harmonises with received conceptions. There are points, for instance, in his presentment of the Platonic doctrine, with which it is easy to disagree; I merely intend to indicate the conception which Pater formed and expressed, the angle at which the idea impinged upon his own mind.

He intended it primarily to be a useful book, an educational work. He says in his preface that his aim was to interest young students of philosophy; and he says at the outset of the book, "The business of the young scholar . . . in reading Plato, is not to take his side in a controversy, to adopt or refute Plato's opinions, to modify, or make apology for, what may seem erratic or impossible in him; still less, to furnish himself with arguments on behalf of some theory or conviction of his own. His duty is rather to follow intelligently, but with strict indifference, the mental process there, as he might witness a game of skill." His own object, therefore, in the book is not primarily philosophical; it is rather critical and historical—to put Plato in his proper place and to see the relation which he bore to his age.

Indeed it would be misleading to speak of Pater as a philosopher in the technical sense of the word, namely, as one who publishes systematic or consecutive thoughts upon the ultimate nature of things. Pater was merely philosophically cultured, and the most we can say of his philosophy is that his mental attitude is to a considerable extent determined by his interest in the study of philosophical opinions. He was, then, a philosopher in the sense that Ruskin, for instance, was not a philosopher; but Pater would not be accepted among critical writers as a philosopher in the technical sense.

It was ingeniously said of Pater, that he was a philo-

sopher who had gone to Italy by mistake instead of to
Germany. There is a real truth in this epigram. He
had a deep-seated sense of the mysterious inner relation of things, an intense desire to discern and disentangle the bare essential motives of life; but
instead of attacking this in the region of pure and
abstract thought, he touched it through the sense of
beauty. It was beauty that seemed to him the most
characteristic, the most significant thing in the world,
that beauty touched with strangeness of which he so
seriously spoke; and his preoccupation was to penetrate the strangeness, to trace the mystery back to
primal emotion, while he watched, with the intensest
eagerness and the most sacred thrill, the rich accumulation of beauty, apprehended and expressed by so many
personalities, such varied natures, which the human race
acquired and made its own, leaving its fine creations to
exist as monuments of its currents and movements,
like the weed-fringed posts that mark the sea-channel
over the estuary's sands; while they gathered year by
year the added beauty of age and association, yet
never losing the pathos, the heart-hunger, the unful-
filled desire, that hangs like a sweet and penetrating
aroma round the beautiful things that men have made
and loved, and have been forced to leave behind them.
The passionate desire to create and express, followed
by the consecration of sorrow and darkness, these two
strains mingled for Pater into a strain of high solemnity
and pathetic sweetness.

But he can hardly be said to have had any philosophical system, just as he himself believed Plato to
have had none. Plato's writings represented to Pater
an atmosphere, not a defined creed. Pater was rather
a psychologist, and it was through the effect of metaphysical ideas upon personality that he approached

philosophy. He was not an abstract thinker; he says, indeed, plainly, " Of course we are not naturally formed to love, or be interested in, or attracted towards, the abstract as such. . . . We cannot love or live upon *genus* and *species*, accident or substance, but for our minds, as for our bodies, need an orchard or a garden, with fruit and roses." But his psychology gave him the power of making metaphysics real to people who are not natur- ally metaphysical, by touching them with a personal appeal, and showing their ethical significance; he translates the pure thought of abstract thinkers into artistic and ethical values. It is interesting, for in- stance, to contrast his development with the develop- ment of such a man as Henry Sidgwick. Both were saved by the uneventful course of academic life from the pressure of hard facts and of social problems. Both began with a metaphysical and a literary bias; but Henry Sidgwick was fitted for abstract speculation, and the literary and artistic interests of his life tended to diminish; whereas in Pater's case the literary and artistic interests developed, and subordinated his meta- physical interests to his artistic prepossessions.

In *Plato and Platonism*, then, Pater is absorbed in the task of bringing out the personality of Plato. This he does with singular skill. He shows that Plato was not an originator of philosophical thought; that it is the form and not the matter that is new; and that his charm lies in his romantic realism, his love of modest and ingenuous youth, his dramatic sense of character; so that, as Pater says, he had a resemblance to Thackeray, and was fully equipped to be a writer of noble fiction. He shows that Plato was in no sense a doctrinaire, but held that ideas and notions are not the consequence of reason but the cause of it. That they are there to be discovered, not non-existent and

capable of being originated; he shows how Plato, in
the *Republic*, was presenting philosophy as an essentially
practical thing, a thing to mould life and conduct, an
escape from the evils of the world—a religion, in fact,
and not a philosophical system. Philosophy is, according to Plato, to teach us how to cultivate the qualities
by which we can obtain a mastery over ourselves, how
to arrive at a kind of musical proportion, the subordination of the parts to the whole. "It is life itself," he
says, "action and character, he proposes to colour; to
get something of that irrepressible conscience of art,
that spirit of control, into the general course of life,
above all into its energetic or impassioned acts."

Thus Plato, according to Pater, is an advocate of
the *immutable*, of law and principle. "Change is the
irresistible law of our being. . . . Change, he protests,
through the power of a true philosophy, shall not be
the law of our being." He shows that Plato was by
constitution an emphatically sensuous nature, deeply
sensible to impressions of beauty, and to emotional
relations with others; but that he regarded the appeal
of the senses as a species of moral education; that the
philosophical learner passed from the particular to the
general, from the love of precise and personal beauty
to the love of the central and inner beauty.

And thus Plato is not so much a teacher as a noble
and inspiriting comrade; those who love Plato do not
sit at his feet and absorb his wisdom, but take service
with him in his adventurous band, journeying from
the familiar scene and the beloved home to the remote
and distant mountains that close the horizon, but from
which there may be a prospect of hidden lands.

The whole book cannot be held to be exactly characteristic of Pater's deliberate style. It is composed
not so much to embody his own dreams as to make a

personality, an age, a spirit, clear to younger minds; but there is a sense of a delighted zest, a blithe freedom about it, as though it were the work of a mind which had escaped from tyrannical impulses and uneasy questionings into a gentle tranquillity of thought. One feels that not only is the subject dear to him, but that those whom he would address are also dear; there is thus an affectionate solicitude, a buoyant easiness, about the book, as of a master speaking simply and unconstrainedly among a band of eager and friendly pupils. The book is full of echoes out of a well-filled mind, of Augustine and Dante, of Shakespeare and Wordsworth. Not only Plato himself, but the other incidental figures are brilliantly touched. Socrates, himself "rude and rough as some failure of his own old sculptor's workshop," yet "everywhere, with what is like a physical passion for what *is*, what is *true*—as one engaged in a sort of religious or priestly concentration of soul on what God really made and meant us to know"; or Pythagoras, that distant legendary figure, with his strange glimpses of pre-existence, emerging as a brilliant, perhaps showy, personality, a mysterious or mystical thaumaturge,—these are sharply and definitely conceived.

Again, there is a beautiful chapter on Lacedaemon, and the decorous, ordered, submissive system of the Dorians, which presented so strong a contrast to the diffuse, unregulated, brilliant spirit of Ionian communities. The Spartan theory of education, with its resemblance to our own English system, developing the individual only in order to subordinate him to the common welfare, repressing all eclectic, all independent qualities, had a potent attraction for Pater's mind, the attraction that all systems have that promise tranquillity and settled instincts as a reward for obedience, for a mind that desires guidance, and to whom personal freedom has brought more anxiety than serenity. The high value of this chapter is that it contrives to invest a system which, barely and unsympathetically described, appears to be ineffably dreary and unpicturesque, with the charm of cheerfulness and quietness so characteristic of communities of a monastic order, a cheerfulness which comes from the removal of personal responsibility, and the substitution of unquestioning obedience—that highest of all luxuries for indecisive and sensitive characters.

The book, then, is a beautiful thing, with a sense of recovered youth blending with an older wisdom about it; a book admirably fitted to attract and instruct an ingenuous mind; but lucid, interesting, and gracious as it is, Pater does not here emerge as the *parfait prosateur*, as Bourget called him; it was no doubt the delight of feeling that in this book he had conferred a real educational benefit upon those youthful spirits to whom his heart went out, that made him rate the book so highly. He did not feel so sure whither the artistic reveries, the metaphysical speculations of his other works might conduct them; but, for all that, criticism is right in setting a higher value upon his more intimate self-revelations, upon the books in which he uttered oracles, rather than on the book where he furthered knowledge.

In the last year of Pater's life he published one of the *Greek Studies*—"The Age of Athletic Prizemen," which we have already considered, and two little sketches of travel—"Some Great Churches in France," which appeared in the *Nineteenth Century* in March and June of that year. "Notre-Dame d'Amiens" is a fine study of a great church, dwelling on the lightness, the brightness, the "immense cheerfulness" of the building.

The only very noteworthy passage is one in which he contrasts Greek and Gothic architecture. He says that in Gothic art "for the mere *melody* of Greek architecture, for the sense as it were of music in the opposition of successive sounds, you got *harmony*, the richer music generated by opposition of sounds in one and the same moment; and were gainers". . . "the vast complexity of the Gothic style seemed, as if consciously, to correspond to the richness, the expressiveness, the thousandfold influence of the Catholic religion."

Again in "Vézelay" (1894) we have a study in contrast, of a "majestic, immoveable" church, which, with "its masses of almost unbroken masonry, its *inertia*," seems to have a certain kinship with imperial Rome. Its almost savage character, he says, is hardly relieved by a great band of energetic, realistic, coarsely executed sculpture, in which demons make merry over the punishment of wickedness : "Bold, crude, original, the work indicates delight in the power of reproducing fact, curiosity in it, but little or no sense of beauty."

But the end was at hand, although there was no hint or foreshadowing of it. Never had Pater been more tranquil, serene, contented, than in these last months. Increasing years, without diminishing strength, concentration, or intellectual force, had brought him nothing but what was good; the respect, the regard, the devotion of friends; the consciousness that he had now a perfect control of his art and its resources. He had many designs and schemes for books that should be written, and there seemed no reason why he should not have many years before him of simple life and congenial activity ; and so we come to his last utterance.

The essay on "Pascal" has a deep significance

among the writings of Pater; it contains, thinly veiled under the guise of criticism, some of his deepest thoughts on the great mystery of life—freewill and necessity—and his views of orthodox theology. It is true that he is nominally justifying Pascal and confuting the Jesuits; but there is a passionate earnestness about his line of argument which shows only too clearly that he was doing what it suited his natural reticence to do—fighting like Teucer under the shield of Ajax, and taking a part, an eager part, in the controversy between Liberalism and Authority.

Moreover, it is his last work; the work on which he was engaged in the last hours of his life; the essay, indeed, never received the last touches of that careful hand, and though substantially complete, it breaks off in the middle of a sentence. This fact—that it was his last deliberate utterance—gives it a special significance; even before he had said his last word on the mystery of life, he knew all that there is to know.

To take the theological side of the essay first, speaking of Pascal's half-contemptuous attempts to arrive at the true definition of theological phrases, Pater thus comments upon the situation :—

"Pascal's charges are those which may seem to lie ready to hand against all who study theology, a looseness of thought and language, that would pass nowhere else, in making what are professedly very fine distinctions; the insincerity with which terms are carefully chosen to cover opposite meanings; the fatuity with which opposite meanings revolve into one another, in the strange vacuous atmosphere generated by professional divines."

"The sin of the Jesuits," he says, "is above all that sin, unpardonable with men of the world *sans peur et sans reproche*, of a lack of self-respect, sins against pride, if the paradox may be allowed, all the undignified faults, in a word, of essentially little people when they interfere in great matters—faults promoted in the direction of the consciences of women and children, weak concessions to weak people who want to be saved in some easy way, quite other than Pascal's high, fine, chivalrous way of gaining salvation."

In these words breathes the accent of the liberal spirit, the spirit which dares to look close into great questions; declines to admit more than it can prove, or at least infer; refuses, at whatever loss of serenity, to formulate its hopes and desires as certainties.

The Jesuit doctrine of sufficient grace is that grace is always vouchsafed in sufficient measure to overcome temptation, if only the spirit chooses to make use of it by the exercise of its free choice.

"This doctrine," says Pater, "is certainly, to use the familiar expression, a very pleasant doctrine conducive to the due feeding of the whole flock of Christ, as being, as assuming them to be, what they really are, at the worst, God's silly sheep."

Pater goes on to say, with an outspokenness which is hardly characteristic of him, that the very opposite doctrine, the Calvinistic doctrine of election both to reprobation and to salvation, would seem to be strikingly confirmed by our own experience. Pascal himself, a visibly elect soul, acting as it were by a certain irresistible impulse of holiness, is an instance in point.

He makes, of course, no attempt at the solution of the insoluble difficulty. But nowhere else in the whole of his writings does he touch on the great dilemma, namely, that our consciousness tells us we are free, our reason that we are bound. He only surveys it from the spectatorial point of view.

"Who," he says, "on a survey of life from outside would willingly lose the dramatic contrasts, the alternating interests,

for which the opposed ideas of freedom and necessity are our
respective points of view ?"

But Pater leaves us in little doubt as to the side on
which his own heart was engaged. It is clear that he
felt that we are not, when our humanity is sifted to
the very bottom, independent beings ; we are deeply
involved and hampered; something outside of us and
anterior to us determines our bent, our very path.

This last deep utterance of Pater's has a strange
significance when taken side by side with the fact so
often stated that he was thinking of the possibility
of receiving Anglican ordination. There could not
possibly be a greater mistake than this supposition.
Perhaps, indeed, there was a region of his mind in
which the idea appealed to him; but deeper down,
in a secret chamber of thought, which in his writings
at all events he did not often visit, lay that consciousness of the hard, dark, bare truth which, if a
man once truly apprehends, prevents him from figuring
as a partisan, except through a certain sophistry, on
the side of authoritative religion.

This is the truth, disguise it as we will, that
religion in its purest form is not a solution of the
world's mystery, but a working theory of morals.
For all religions, even Christianity itself, tend to
depend upon certain assumptions, such as the con-
tinuance, in some form or other, of our personal
identity after death, of which no scientific evidence
is forthcoming. We may assume it, yielding to a
passionate intuition, but nothing can prevent it from
being an assumption, an intuition, which may perhaps transcend reason, but cannot wholly satisfy it.
And thus, however impassioned, however transcendent
that intuition may be, there must always remain a

certain element of doubt, in all sincere minds, as to the absolute certainty of the assumption. Thus there must lie, in all reasoning men's hearts, a streak of agnosticism. The triumph of faith can never, until faith melts into certainty, be of the same quality as the triumph of reason; and it is upon the proportion of doubt to faith in any man's mind that his religious attitude depends. There is little question as to which way Pater's sympathies and hopes inclined; but this essay clearly reveals that the doubt was there.

He touches with deep sympathy the strange and sad withdrawal of Pascal from the world; his attempt, under the pressure of a painful and unmanning disease, to find solace in asceticism, renunciation, and the practice of austere pieties; it seems strange to Pater to find that Pascal never fell under the aesthetic charm of the rites of the Catholic Church, but found "a certain weariness, a certain puerility, a certain unprofitableness in them." "He seems," he adds, "to have little sense of the beauty of holiness," but to be absorbed by a "sombre, trenchant, precipitous philosophy."

He treats of Pascal from the literary side with a whole-hearted admiration. He says that he made the French language "as if by a new creation, what it has remained—a pattern of absolutely unencumbered expressiveness." He dwells on the fragrant charm, the naturalness of the *Letters*, proceeding from one who was hardly a student, knowing but two or three great books. And the *Pensées* he considers to be pure inspirations "penetrating what seemed hopelessly dark." How could the *Pensées* be more nobly summarised than as "those great fine sayings which seem to betray by their depth of sound the vast unseen hollow places of nature, of humanity, just beneath one's feet"? They seem to him to combine faultless expression, perfect economy of statement, marvellous suggestiveness, with a "somewhat Satanic intimacy" with the weaknesses of the human heart.

What kept Pascal from scepticism, or, rather, what threw him into religion, was a bewildered, a terrified apprehension of the strange inconsistency of human nature, the blending of meanness and greatness which everywhere appears.

We may consider this essay, then, as Pater's most deliberate utterance on ethical things. It reveals him, I think, as a deep though unwilling sceptic; it shows a soul athirst yet unsatisfied; it shows that the region of beauty, both in art and religion, in which he strove to live, was but an outer paradise in which he found what peace he could; but in the innermost shrine all is dark and still.

On leaving London, Pater had settled, in 1893, in a house in St. Giles', Oxford. It is a quiet house with a plastered front of some antiquity, with a pleasant row of trees in front of it; at the left is a little passage leading to the back of the house. The inner arch is surmounted with a quaint carved face. Here he settled with his sisters in great contentment.

The President of Magdalen, Mr. T. H. Warren, speaking of the later Oxford days, writes :—

" One would have said that there was a kind of placid piety, an inner content, which somehow manifested itself in him. He did not talk a great deal, yet always enough. What I think struck me most about him was a sort of gentleness in his whole manner, in perception and predilection, almost at times a softness,—and yet it was balanced by hardness of decision too. He was a very familiar figure, with his pale face, strong jaw, heavy, chopped, German-looking moustache, tall hat and apple-green tie. He was often seen walking, and latterly he rather laboured in his walk, which gave, rightly or wrongly, the idea of conscious or half-conscious suffering. . . . At the Dante Society he did not say much, but what always struck me was that he spoke with a certain authority and a strong common sense ; and, moreover, with what appeared a personal and natural knowledge of what a poet or a literary artist in his temperament and habits really is. . . .

"It seemed to me that he cultivated a wise, grave passiveness, a gentle susceptibility, a kind of soft impressionability ; that he tried to keep, and did keep, a sort of *bloom* upon his mind. I never remember a single unkind criticism or remark. . . . My opinion of him is rather an impression than an opinion, and that is, I think, what he would himself have wished—and what is fairest too.

"Can I put it in a few words ? He expressed life for himself and to others in terms of sensations, of impressions. These he might analyse, combine, and re-combine, but together they formed his working synthesis. I did not really know him in the earlier days, when in his written work the sensuousness and the referability of everything to sensation was so avowed. I only knew him well much later when he had become a kind of quietist : what the real man was I could not say."

In the spring of 1894 Pater went to Glasgow to receive the honorary degree of LL.D., a little piece of recognition which pleased him, and took the opportunity of visiting some of the Northern Cathedrals. In the summer of the same year he was for the first time in his life seriously ill. He had an attack of rheumatic fever and was confined to his bed. But he made an apparent recovery, and became convalescent. He was allowed to leave his bed and come downstairs. He was full of cheerfulness and interest, though he was feeling weak ; it is certain, however, that there was something organically wrong, though he allowed himself, with the instinct of one who enjoyed the ordinary routine of life to the full, and who was impatient of invalid conditions, to resume his activities too soon. Still there seemed no reason to suppose that he was acting imprudently. He was working at the lecture on Pascal, which was to have been delivered in July, when, in consequence of writing too near to an open window, he had an attack of pleurisy, which still further reduced his strength. Again he became convalescent, and left his room on July 29 without ill effects. But on the morning of Monday, July 30, 1894, at ten o'clock, on coming downstairs, he had a sudden attack of heart failure, and died apparently without suffering. If he had lived five days longer he would have completed his fifty-fifth year. He was buried in the Holywell cemetery at Oxford, in the presence of many of his old friends. It is melancholy to feel that in all probability his life might have been prolonged for some years, if he had but realised how much reduced in strength he was. But it was the happiest kind of end that could befall a man of Pater's sensitive and apprehensive temperament. He had always, from his earliest years, been much preoccupied with the thought of death, and even with the effort to reconcile himself to it. It was strange and beautiful that it should, after all, have befallen him so quietly and simply. He felt no shadow of death, no mournful forebodings of mortality. He had won a secure fame, he was surrounded with respect and affection, he had fulfilled in patience and with much quiet happiness a great task; and so with no decay of faculty, no diminution of zest and enthusiasm, no melancholy foreboding, death came to him as a quiet friend and beckoned him smilingly away.

Yet as we realise that this wistful, this inquisitive spirit had indeed drawn near to the gate, through which he had seen others pass, had indeed endured the

passage, upon the incidents and impressions of which
he had often meditated with an intense and reverent
curiosity, the imagination torments and perplexes
itself with the wonder as to what the end or the
awakening may have been, whether indeed he ever
knew, in some moment of swimming gaze and darkened
eyes, that he should not return to life and daylight.
We find our minds dwelling upon the words with
which he ended the finest of all his essays, that on
"Leonardo da Vinci," written twenty-five years before.
We lose ourselves "in speculating how one who had
been always so desirous of beauty, but desired it always
in such definite and precise forms, as hands or flowers
or hair, looked forward now into the vague land, and
experienced the last curiosity."

CHAPTER VII

PERSONAL CHARACTERISTICS

In younger days Pater was refined and dignified in appearance; there is an early photograph of him, shortly after he took his degree, with a soft eye, a serious gentle look, with regular and rounded features.[1] But this altered in later years; he became graver and heavier of aspect, and his face took on a character that has been described as "Japanese"; the pallor of his complexion, like old ivory, became more marked; but his eyes were his most eloquent feature, of a light hazel tint, almost grey-green, which lit up with an impressive light of animation and kindness when he was moved.

He was in later life slow of movement, bent, sad of aspect, except when particularly stirred, and somewhat sedentary in appearance. Yet he was broad-shouldered, strongly-built, sturdy, and gave an impression of soundness, and even toughness of constitution. His great pale face, with the strong lower jaw and carefully trimmed moustache, gave him something of the air of a retired military man. There was an impression sometimes of languor about him. He had to strangers, at first sight, in later years, a

[1] There is a portrait of him, a drawing by Simeon Solomon, made in 1872, now in the possession of Mr. Herbert Horne. There is also another drawing, a lithograph, by Mr. Rothenstein, included in the Oxford Portraits. Neither of these is considered wholly satisfactory by those who knew Pater best.

fatigued, faded, lustreless air, as of a caged creature. But this, I learn from those who knew him best, was in reality a false impression. He was undoubtedly robust; he was a patient, an unwearying traveller, often walking long distances without fatigue, and bearing uncomplainingly the extreme of Italian heat. But, like all impressionable, perceptive, artistic temperaments, his physical strength was apt to ebb and flow with his inner mood; when he was pleased, interested, delighted, he was also equable, animated, alert. When he was aware that he was expected to fulfil anticipations, conscious of social strain, uninterested, he became melancholy, drooping, unstrung. To any one introduced to him for the first time he at once gave the impression of great gentleness and sympathy. There was nothing awe-inspiring about him but his reputation. His low deferential voice, his shy smile, the delicate phrasing of his sentences, his obvious interest in the temperament of his companion, gave the feeling of great and sincere humility. He was, too, singularly easy and accessible; he had no desire to keep a conversation in his own hands, or to claim attention for his opinions. He had rather a delicate power of encouraging confidence and frankness. One realised at once that one was in the presence of a man of subtle sensibilities, anxious, not of set purpose but from considerate instinct, to do the fullest justice to the feelings of his companion, and to give him his undivided attention. This came from a fine simplicity of nature, from a character that made no egotistical demands; he seemed to expect and to require little from life, but to be full of a quiet gratitude for such delight as came naturally in his way.

He arrayed himself with scrupulous neatness, and always dressed for Hall. He invariably wore a tall hat, and carried the neatest of gold-topped umbrellas. His gait was peculiar : he had a slight stoop, and dragged one foot slightly, advancing with a certain delicacy. He disliked stopping to talk to people, and often was at some pains not to appear to recognise them ; he had a peculiar courteous gesture of the hand, if recognition was inevitable, by which he paid a certain tribute of courtesy, and yet contrived to indicate that he wished to be unmolested. He was shy in large mixed assemblies, but his shyness did not make him silent or abrupt. He was apt to talk, gently and persistently, of trivial topics, using his conversation rather as a shield against undue intimacy.

People on first meeting him were sometimes struck with the extraordinary conventionality of his manners and conversation in society ; but this almost oppressive suavity melted into a gentle and sympathetic kindness on further acquaintance. A friend, writing to Miss Pater after her brother's death, spoke of

"his kindness, his sweetness, his gentle and amiable wearing of all his great gifts, his happy and gracious willingness to give all around him the enjoyment of them."

Another friend of his writes :—

"The only attitude I ever observed in Pater, the only mood I saw him in, was a sort of weary courtesy with which he used to treat me, with somehow a deep kindness shining through. It was as though he would have liked to lavish sympathy and even affection, but was frightened of the responsibility and unequal to the effort. He seemed to me, if I may use an allegory, to point to a sack of treasure, and say,—'That is yours, if you like to take it ; I am only sorry that I am too tired myself to rise and place it in your hands.'"

But, on the other hand, Dr. Bussell, the closest com-

panion in the later years, writes of the side of himself
that Pater turned to the nearer circle:—

"His ordinary talk . . . was the happiest blending of
seriousness and mirth, of deep feeling and a sort of childlike
glee in the varying surfaces of things."

This subdued air came to a certain extent from the
circumstances of his life, but still more from a deep-
seated reclusiveness, rather than humility of nature.
Indeed, it may be said that, with all his gentleness, he
was not innately humble. What often appeared to
be humility was, in reality, an intense dislike of
opposition. A consciousness of antagonism irritated
him so intensely, that he often preferred to withdraw
both what he had said and written, rather than pro-
voke contradiction and argument. It was not that he
was diffident about his intuitions; he was rather
diffident about his power of defending and recommend-
ing them. He was little inclined to dogmatise, and
realised most sympathetically the differences of temperament; but the path which he had chosen was the
only path for him; and though he might seem to yield
to argument and remonstrance, he was never converted, except by reflection. He was probably never
fully appreciated at Oxford. Busy, effective, academical natures tended to think of him as a secluded
dreamer of dreams; his fame grew so insensibly and
secretly, and was, even so, confined so much to the
συνετοί, the connoisseurs, that there never came that
revulsion of feeling that has sometimes lifted a man
suddenly on to a pinnacle of unquestioned reputation.
Moreover, it is fair to say that the air of the Universities is not at the present moment favourable to the
pursuit of *belles lettres* and artistic philosophies. The
praise of academical circles is reserved at the present

time for people of brisk bursarial and business qualifi-
cations, for men of high technical accomplishment,
for exact researchers, for effective teachers of prescribed subjects, for men of acute and practical minds,
rather than for men of imaginative qualities. This is
the natural price that must be paid for the increased
efficiency of our Universities, though it may be
regretted that they maintain so slight a hold upon the
literary influences of the day. The whole atmosphere
is, in fact, sternly critical, and the only work which
is emphatically recognised and approved is the work
which makes definite and unquestionable additions to
the progress of exact sciences.

A genial epigrammatist once said that if a man
desired to court unpopularity in academical circles he
had but to enjoy an outside reputation, to write a good
literary style, and to make it his business to see something of undergraduates, to gain his end with entire
celerity.

There is some truth in the contention. The erudite
world is apt to think that a reputation acquired with
the general public by literary accomplishments is a
second-rate sort of affair, and only to be gained by
those who are not sufficiently hard-headed and exact
to win academical repute. A man, too, who betrays
an interest in the younger members of the community
is thought to be slightly abnormal, and either to be
actuated by a vague sentimentality, or else to be
desirous of receiving the admiration of immature
minds, which he cannot win from more mature
intellects.

This atmosphere, these conditions, Pater accepted
with the gentle outward deference that was characteristic of him; he had no taste for the warm luxuriance
of coteries; he had no sort of desire to label with

contemptuous names those who must have appeared to
him deaf and blind to the subtle and beautiful effects
that made the substance of his own life.

It seemed a curious irony of fate which planted
Pater in a college which for years enjoyed a robust
pre-eminence for athletic triumphs, together with a
reputation for wholesome turbulence. But it may be
said that such an atmosphere was not wholly uncongenial to Pater. Though he had no sort of pro-
ficiency in athletics, and though he was pre-eminently
peaceable in disposition, he had, as I have said, a genuine
and deep admiration for strongly developed physical
vigour, while he had little of the sensitive disciplinary
instinct that feels the frank display of youthful ebullience a kind of slur upon the privileges of constituted
authority. No one was more anxious than Pater, in
a disciplinary crisis, to give a case a fair hearing, and
to condone as far as possible an outbreak that was
thoughtless rather than deliberate. In all cases where
there was a question of the infliction of punishment for
some breach of discipline, Pater was always on the
side of mercy. And this was with no wish to preserve
his own dignity by temporising with the disorderly
section. He was always a loyal and faithful supporter
of authority, while he was anxious that a case should
not be judged with the undue sternness that the sense
of outraged dignity tends to bring with it. As Dr.
Bussell wrote:—

" Naturally inclined to a certain rigour in discipline, he
was full of excuse for individual cases ; and regretted, and
thought over stern measures more than most members of a
governing body can afford to do."

Apocryphal stories are related of him, such as his
excuse for the rowdiness of undergraduates after

Hall, that they reminded him of playful young tigers that had just been fed; or his supposed remark about bonfires in Brasenose quad, that he did not object to them because they lighted up the spire of St. Mary's so beautifully. These were, of course, intended to represent the imperturbable search for beautiful impressions in the most incongruous circumstances; but they represent, too, a half-truth, namely, a real and vital charity of nature, inclined to condone, and even to sympathise with, the manifestations of natural feeling, however personally inconvenient.

Perhaps the playful irony, the light-handed humour, which was to Pater a deliberate shield against the roughness of the world, tended to obscure his deep seriousness of nature, his devotedly religious spirit. He sympathised, it is true, with all humanity with a largeness which is surprising in a man of such sensitive and secluded constitution. He had a determination, remarkable in a man of delicate organisation, to see the world as it really was, to admire what was vigorous and natural and vital in it. He had no wish to create for himself an unreal paradise, to suppose the world to be other than it appeared, or to drown the insistent cries that reached him in a web of blurred impression or uncertain sound. He admired what was joyful and brave and strong. Had he been of a more alert physical constitution he would have thrown himself, we may safely assert, into the pursuit of athletics ardently and eagerly. As he could not, he contented himself with admiring the youthful exuberance of activity, and, true to his nature, with disentangling as far as he could the fibre of beauty which ran for him through the universe. But in all this he was akin and not alien to the insouciant and pleasure-loving spirit of youth.

He was by nature an extremely reticent man; he never seemed to think that his ideas were likely to command attention or his personality to cause interest. He wrote very few letters and never kept a diary. His whole attitude to the world and its concerns was the attitude of a spectator, and even his closest and nearest relationships with others could not win him from his isolation; he could be kind, courteous, considerate, and sincere; but he could not be intimate; he always guarded his innermost heart.

He was very loath to express his own personal view of a matter, especially if it involved taking any credit to himself. But a friend remembers that he was once talking of the artistic perceptions of Ruskin, and said suddenly with a show of impatience, "I cannot believe that Ruskin saw more in the church of St. Mark than I do."

His courteous deference, to both old and young alike, was very remarkable. He would agree gently with the crudest expressions of opinion, "No doubt! I had never thought of it in that light!" But he could occasionally fire up when some deeply felt opinion of his own was challenged. Mr. Ainslie remembers being in his company when some one spoke disparagingly of Flaubert. He came suddenly out of his shell, and spoke with great emotion and much wealth of illustration.

Though Pater was never unkind, he could give a pungent judgment on occasions. The conversation, in his presence, had once turned upon H. A. J. Munro, and a man was mentioned with whom Munro was intimate, and with whom he often associated, who was distinguished rather for a mundane interest in affairs and for a devotion to sociable and convivial enjoyment than for any interest in literature or scholarship.

Surprise was expressed at this friendship. "I should not have thought they had anything in common," said one of those present. "Do you think that is so?" said Pater, "I always felt that there was a good deal of the *mahogany-table* element in Munro." This is a just judgment, which, though ironically expressed, exhibits a considerable penetration on the part of Pater, in the case of a man of whom he knew but little.

He was extraordinarily loyal to his friends. He spoke once with great gravity and seriousness of one whom he had known, whom he thought to be drifting into dangerous courses, and expressed a deep desire to help or warn him, or, at all events, to get a warning conveyed to him. His confidant tells me that he never saw him so deeply moved and distressed as on this occasion, as he tried to devise some way of bringing conviction home to the unhappy object of his anxiety.

His tendency indeed was always to mitigate harsh judgments, to appreciate the good points of those with whom he was brought into contact. He had indeed a great eye for little individualities and peculiarities, with a gentle enjoyment of the manifestation of foibles; but it was always an indulgent and a tender attitude. And it may be said that it is rare to find one so perceptive of the most delicate and subtle shades of temperament, who was yet so uniformly charitable and kind, so determined to see the best side of every one.

Pater kept himself severely aloof from the current thought of the day, but with characteristic reticence never adopted the position of an opponent. He took no interest in scientific movements or discoveries, and merely left such questions alone.

serve a dignity of deportment. At such moments a look of silent and rapturous appreciation may pass between two kindred spirits ; such, in its fineness and secrecy, is the humour of Pater's writings, and presupposes a sympathetic understanding between writer and reader.

Dr. Bussell, writing of the apparent contrast between the solemnity of his writings and his demeanour to his closest friends, writes :—

"To a certain extent, but to a certain extent only, these (writings) may be taken as an index to his character, as unveiling the true man. But to those who knew him as he lived among us here, they seemed a sort of disguise. There was the same tenderness, the same tranquillizing repose about his conversation that we find in his writings ; the same care-fulness in trifles, and exactness of expression. But his written works betray little trace of that childlike simplicity, that naïve joyousness, that never-wearying pleasure in animals and their ways,—that grave yet half-amused seriousness, also childlike, in which he met the events of the daily routine."

Those who did not know him personally have sup-posed him to be a man of a strained and affected solemnity. The exact opposite was the truth. Pater did not despise the day of small things. He loved easy talk and simple laughter. He had a relish for small jokes. He loved plays that made him laugh. Such performances as Gilbert and Sullivan's operas were his delight, and a friend who accompanied him to *Ruddigore* said that it was delightful to see the whole-hearted and childlike enjoyment to which he surrendered himself. Mr. Gosse went with him to Mr. Pinero's *Magistrate*, and remembers him convulsed with overwhelming laughter. In his own home he used to discourse with intense gravity, mingled with great bursts of laughter, of the adventures of a set

of entirely fictitious relatives. Again, he took a delighted pleasure in the ways and mannerisms of his
acquaintances. Mr. Gosse remembers how admirably
he used to imitate Mark Pattison's speech and peevish
intonation. This was best exemplified in the imaginary
dialogue which Pater used to render, supposed to take
place between the Rector of Lincoln and a burglar
who had invaded his house: "I am a poor old man.
Look at me, you can see that I am a very poor man.
Go across to Fowler—he is rich, and all his plate is
real. He is a very snug fellow, Fowler!" This was
a really admirably dramatic performance, so dramatic
that Pater appeared to be quite convinced of its truth.

Pater had an unceasing delight in watching the ways
and habits of pet animals. His own domestic cats,
indeed, were kept and lovingly tended, till from age
and disease, they had nearly lost all semblance to the
feline form. He was deeply conscious of the charm
of seeing these bright creatures so close at hand, with
the extraordinary relation that may exist, such perfect
confidence, such unrestrained affection, while yet there
is no communication of thought, and so little comprehension on either side of what is really passing in the
mind. He was strangely attracted by the mysterious
tie, so close and, in a way, so intimate, and yet with
so little mutual understanding, and accompanied by
such isolation. He was particularly fond of cats, their
dainty ways, their graceful attitudes ; and aware too
of the refined selfishness, so different from the eager
desire to please of the dog; the cat, intent on its own
business, using human beings to minister to its needs,
making its own arrangements, giving or withholding
its company, with no idea of obedience or subservience
or dependence; but just living gracefully and indo-
lently in the houses of men, because it suits its con-

venience to do so. All this, together with its dramatic mystery, its intent secretiveness, its whimsical mirth, its charming solemnity, had an unfailing pleasure for Pater. He was always strangely drawn too, with a mixture of curiosity and indignation, by the sight of those collections of incongruous animals known as Happy Families that are to be seen in gregarious resorts ; he would linger about them, expressing his indignation, yet always ending by contributing liberally to their maintenance.

In conversation, especially in earlier days, Pater adopted a consistent and deliberate irony of speech which was such as often to baffle even his intimate friends. He delighted in paradox, and in a kind of whimsical perversity. He would dwell upon the unessential attributes of a scene, a personality, a book, when a serious judgment was desired. And this, combined as it was with a serious, grave, and almost gloomy manner, completed the mystification.

He was fond, as I have said, of insisting upon some altogether unimportant detail on these occasions ; he used to pretend that he shut his eyes in crossing Switzerland, on his journeys to and from Italy, so as not to see the "horrid pots of blue paint," as he called the Swiss lakes. He would profess himself unable to read the books of a person whose name or personal appearance distressed him. The celebrated story, which is widely current about him as to the examination in which he took a part, is characteristic of the same mood. He was supposed to have looked over a paper, but when the examiners met he seemed to have kept no record of his impressions ; to assist his recollection the names of the candidates were read over, but he seemed to be unable to connect any ideas with any of them until the name Sanctuary appeared, at which he visibly brightened,

and said that he was now sure he had looked over
the papers because he remembered that he liked the
name.

Probably the habit arose from the fact that he was
of a shy and sensitive temperament, and that to give a
real and serious opinion was a trial to him. He disliked the possibility of dissent or disapproval, and took
refuge in this habit of irony, so as to baffle his hearers
and erect a sort of fence between them and his own
personality.

But partly too he was undoubtedly aware, in his
earlier days, that the expectation of conversational
friandises amused and delighted his hearers. He was
rather the spoilt child of the intellectual circle in
which he lived, and it is held by some that he rather
presumed on the indulgence of his friends in this
respect.

Mr. Basil Champneys, for instance, recollects how
he was dining in company with Pater at Professor
Bywater's, about the year 1875, with a small party.
The conversation turned on George Eliot, and Pater
announced that he did not think much of George Eliot
as a writer. "It is impossible," he said, "to value a
writer all of whose characters are practically identical.
What," he said, "is Maggie Tulliver but Tito in petti-
coats?" Such a criticism is of course purely perverse,
and contains no germ of critical seriousness.

The same tendency is reflected in the peevish mono-
logue, attributed by tradition to Mark Pattison, and
often delightedly repeated by Pater himself. The
question of possible travelling-companions was being
discussed, when the Rector broke out with : "I would
not travel with Pater for anything! He would say the
steamboat was not a steamboat, and that Calais was
not Calais!"

The example that he set was somewhat contagious. Those affected by it became the most subjective of critics, and acquired the superficial conversational method, which consisted in speaking of serious things on social occasions as if they had no seriousness, and of diligently searching for the ridiculous aspect that they could be found to bear. There came a certain reaction at a later date against this style of conversation, until the flippant treatment of topics, however superficially amusing, came to be regarded with perhaps undue impatience. But the fact remains that Pater was in ordinary talk, through early years, *un vrai moqueur*, while the seriousness of his demeanour lent a certain piquancy to his paradoxical talk which had a distinct charm. In this respect, indeed, the caricature of Pater in the pages of the *New Republic* gives an entirely wrong impression. In the *New Republic* Mr. Rose is made to talk as though he were uttering his secret thoughts, *dicenda tacenda locutus*, with entire indifference to the tone of the audience that surrounded him. This is a hopeless misconception of Pater's ordinary ways.

There are two or three anecdotes which survive which aptly illustrate the same tendency. I do not know to what extent these reminiscences are coloured by the legendary element, but they are contemporary stories which have survived, and are therefore worth repeating. He was asked, for instance, whether he did not find his College work a great burden to him. He replied with inimitable gravity, "Well, not so much as you might think. The fact is that most of our men are fairly well-to-do, and it is not necessary that they should learn very much. At some Colleges I am told that certain of the young men have a genuine love for learning; if that were so here, it would be quite

N

too dreadful." He sighed, and looked sadly at his auditor.

On another occasion it is said that, when advising a man what to read for Greats, Pater said : "I cannot advise you to read any special books ; the great thing is to read authors *whole* ; read Plato *whole* ; read Kant *whole* ; read Mill *whole*."

Again, though the following is probably to be regarded as legendary, it is said that he once, in a lecture, announced that in certain aspects we might be justified in regarding religion as a beautiful disease. This remark was quoted by an undergraduate to his parent with the substitution of the word "loathsome" for "beautiful." The parent wrote indignantly to Pater to ask if it was right that such opinions should be expressed by a tutor to undergraduates. Pater, according to his own account, replied that he did not think he could have used the word "loathsome." He might, he said, have used the word "beautiful"— "a beautiful disease." "The parent," he added, "expressed himself entirely reassured and satisfied by the explanation." [1]

He went to see a rather elderly game of hockey played by middle-aged performers, and, after a moment of silence, said softly to his companion : "Come away ; I think we ought to go on ; it seems hardly fair to look at them."

But the habit of indulging in ironical or reckless paradox had its dangerous side. There was at Oxford in the days of Pater's early residence a certain aesthetic

[1] The origin of this story is no doubt to be found on p. 217 of the 1889 edition of the *Appreciations*, in the suppressed essay on "Aesthetic Poetry." "That monastic religion of the Middle Age was, in fact, in many of its bearings, like a beautiful disease or disorder of the senses."

movement, a species of renaissance, in which the creed
of beauty was strongly insisted upon. In some members
of the circle that was thus affected, this resulted in much
extravagance of thought; and in some it had even
worse results in loosening the principles of morality,
and judging action by the canons of what was held to be
beautiful. It is a difficult subject to treat discreetly,
because the *epigoni* of the school, in certain notorious
instances, ended in complete moral and social shipwreck.
With the extravagances and excesses of the school it
is needless to say that Pater, a man of scrupulous conscience and a high standard of moral delicacy, had not
the slightest sympathy; but his love of paradox, his
recklessness of irony, unquestionably led him to say
things which could be unhappily distorted and mis-
applied, and which, not in his own case, but in the case
of those who heard and exaggerated them, were capable of being construed in a serious light, and the
utterance of which may be said to have justified both
anxiety and distress. Here, as elsewhere, the true
Pater is to be seen in his writings, and not in his ironical *dicta*. And any careful student of his deliberate
thoughts finds no difficulty in discerning the delicacy
and the loftiness of his view. He refused, it is true, to
take a conventional view of the principles of art; but
though the essential purity of art can be distorted into
a wild appetite for beautiful impressions and sensual
experience, it can yet be safeguarded and kept in a
high and austere region, in which the lower impulse
is entirely inconsistent with the grave appreciation of
beauty.

In the aesthetic movement, Pater concerned himself
solely with the doctrine; but at the same time it is
undeniably true that the leaders of a movement are
always judged by the extravagances of their followers;

and the anxiety and even suspicion with which Pater's
views were at one time regarded in Oxford, were due
to the fact that those with whom he was in a certain
sense in sympathy on the higher aesthetic grounds,
applied the doctrine of beauty to a recklessness of
practice which Pater not only condemned, but the contemplation of which both disgusted and appalled him.
It is better to have no misconception on this point.
It is as unfair to think of Pater as in sympathy with
the decadent school, as it is to attribute to the original
teachers of Predestination the immoral distortion of the
doctrines which disgraced some of their fanatical sec-
taries. When the whole movement has, so to speak,
shaken down; when we can look dispassionately at
the part which the aesthetic school has played in the
mental development of the age, we shall be able, while
we condemn whole-heartedly the excesses of the advanced disciples, to discern the part that Pater and the
other leaders of the movement played in setting the
deliberate appreciation of beauty, the sedulous training
of the perceptions in the discrimination of the subtle
effects of impassioned art, in its right place among the
forces which tend to the ennobling of human character
and temperament.

Having thus drawn out, as far as possible, what
Pater's ethical creed was not, let us try to indicate
the nature and movement of his religious life. He
began, it is plain, by feeling the strong aesthetic attraction of the accessories of religion; probably he
did not disentangle the elements of religious faith from
the effect which great churches, solemn ceremonial,
ecclesiastical music, and hieratic pomp had upon his
mind. As Jowett is once, in early days, reported
to have said to him somewhat irritably, at the close
of a discussion, "Mr. Pater, you seem to think that

religion is all idolatry!" But as soon as Pater plunged into the study of metaphysics, he found that philosophy began to act as a solvent upon his creed; he still had a bias towards the expression of religious truth; and his half-formed idea of becoming a Unitarian minister, which, as I have said, was suggested in all probability by the career of Coleridge, was the outcome of this mood.

After this impulse, if it was ever so much as an impulse, died away, he seems to have been content for some years to suspend his judgment. He even, both in public and in private, used expressions which indicated an attitude of definite hostility to the Christian position. He was immersed in artistic conceptions, and in practical work; but as he grew older the old associations began to reassert themselves; he found, like so many people of speculative temperament, who set out on a philosophical quest with an impatience of received traditions and conventional opinion, that there was far more truth in the accumulated treasures of human thought, simple and in many ways contradictory as they appeared, than he had originally believed. As he wrote once, in one of his reviews for the *Guardian*, " the religious, the Catholic, ideal, . . . the only mode of poetry realizable by the poor."

He discovered afresh the tranquillising influence of a direct faith on quiet people—of the type that he described in another review; speaking of sacristans as "simple people coming and going there, devout, or at least on devout business, with half-pitched voices, not without touches of kindly humour, in what seems to express like a picture the most genial side, midway between the altar and the home, of the ecclesiastical life." And thus the old quiet consecration of life by faith, not very confident perhaps, hardly more than

a sacred hope of beautiful and tender possibilities, re-
asserted itself.

As Lady Dilke wrote of a talk with him in the
later years :—

"Pater came and sate with me till dinner-time. We had
been talking before that on the exclusive cultivation of the
memory in modern teaching as tending to destroy the power
of thought, by sacrificing the attitude of meditation to that
of perpetual apprehension. When the others left we went
on talking of the same matter, but on different lines. Thence
we came to how it might be possible, under present conditions
of belief, to bring people up not as beasts but as men by the
endeavour to train feeling and impart sentiments as well as
information. He looks for an accession of strength to the
Roman Church, and thinks that if it would abandon its folly
in political and social intrigue, and take up the attitude of
a purely spiritual power, it would be, if not the best thing
that could happen, at any rate better than the selfish vulgarity
of the finite aims and ends which stand in the place of an
ideal in most lives now. He has changed a great deal, as I
should think for the better, and is a stronger man."

Pater spoke, indeed, as I conceive, very plainly in
one place—the review of *Robert Elsmere*—of what was
the inner attitude of his mind :—

"*Robert Elsmere* was a type of a large class of minds which
cannot be sure that the sacred story is true. It is philosophical, doubtless, and a duty to the intellect to recognise
our doubts, to locate them, perhaps to give them practical
effect. It may be also a moral duty to do this. But then
there is also a large class of minds which cannot be sure it is
false—minds of very various degrees of conscientiousness and
intellectual power, up to the highest. They will think those
who are quite sure it is false, unphilosophical through lack of
doubt. For their part, they make allowance in their scheme
of life for a great possibility, and with some of them that
bare concession of possibility (the subject of it being what it

is) becomes the most important fact in the world. The recognition of it straightway opens wide the door to hope and love ; and such persons are, as we fancy they always will be, the nucleus of a Church. Their particular phase of doubt, of philosophic uncertainty, has been the secret of millions of good Christians, multitudes of worthy priests. They knit themselves to believers, in various degrees, of all ages."

And thus he came both to feel and to express a deep and sincere sympathy with the Christian point of view ; *Marius* reveals most subtly the closeness of this approximation ; but it may be seen, in scattered hints and touches, through all his later writings. Speaking, for instance, of the death of Socrates he wrote that the "details, as one cannot but observe in passing, which leave those famous hours, even for purely human, or say ! pagan dignity and tenderness, wholly incomparable to one sacred scene to which they have sometimes been compared." A friend of Pater's tells me that the present Bishop of Birmingham, Dr. Gore, went to the Brasenose Church Society to read a paper on the Blessed Trinity, and was rather taken aback to find Pater in the chair. "However, he proved to be an admirable chairman, directing the discussion after the paper, and checking anything approaching irreverence."

He wrote Mrs. Humphry Ward a very interesting letter on December 23, 1885, on receiving from her as a Christmas gift her newly published translation of *Amiel's Journal*. After congratulating her on the admirable literary grace of the translation, he continued :—

" I find a store of general interest in *Amiel*, (take at random, *e.g.*, the shrewd criticism of Quinet,) which must attract all those who care for literature ; while for the moralist and the student of religion he presents the additional attraction of yet another thoroughly original and individual witness to experiences on the subject they care most for. For myself, I gather from your well-meditated introduction, that I shall think, on finishing the book, that there was still something *Amiel* might have added to those elements of natural religion, (so to call it, for want of a better expression,) which he was able to accept, at times with full belief, and always with the sort of hope which is a great factor in life. To my mind, the beliefs, and the function in the world, of the historic church, form just one of those obscure but all-important possibilities, which the human mind is powerless effectively to dismiss from itself ; and might wisely accept, in the first place, as a workable hypothesis. The supposed facts on which Christianity rests, utterly incapable as they have become of any ordinary test, seem to me matters of very much the same sort of assent we give to any assumption, in the strict and ultimate sense, moral. The question whether those facts were real will, I think, always continue to be what I should call one of the *natural* questions of the human mind."

In connection with this frame of mind we may quote an interesting passage which occurs in the *Greek Studies* ("The Bacchanals of Euripides"). He is speaking of Euripides, at the end of a long life of varied emotion and experience ; he says :—

"Writing in old age, he is in that subdued mood, a mood not necessarily sordid, in which (the shudder at the nearer approach of the unknown world coming over him more frequently than of old) accustomed ideas, conformable to a sort of common sense regarding the unseen, oftentimes regain what they may have lost, in a man's allegiance. It is a sort of madness, he begins to think, to differ from the received opinions thereon. Not that he is insincere or ironical, but that he tends, in the sum of probabilities, to dwell on their more peaceful side ; to sit quiet, for the short remaining time, in the reflexion of the more cheerfully lighted side of things ; and what is accustomed—what holds of familiar usage— comes to seem the whole essence of wisdom, on all subjects ;

and the well-known delineation of the vague country, in
Homer or Hesiod, one's best attainable mental outfit, for the
journey thither."

This is no doubt a true picture of the writer's own
inner mood, a forecast of the later years in which the
excitement of the quest for new ideas, new experiences
dies down ; and a man begins to rediscover for himself
the humanity, the reality, of the old and constant
stock of mortal tradition ; the thoughts that have
tortured, comforted, attracted, satisfied the great company of mankind.

When he lived in London he was fond of attending
St. Paul's Cathedral, St. Alban's, Holborn, and other
high Anglican Churches ; and he was sometimes seen
at the Carmelites' Church in Kensington ; but there
is no sort of evidence that he had any thought of
Anglican orders, or that he was tending towards
Roman Catholicism, He found in religion a deep and
tranquillising force, and recognised the religious instinct, the intuitions of faith, as a Divine influence
even more direct and unquestionable than the artistic
or the intellectual influence. And thus we may think
of him as one who, though his intellectual subtlety
prevented his aiming at any very precise definition of
his creed, was yet deeply penetrated by the perfect
beauty and holiness of the Christian ideal, and reposed
in trembling faith on 'the bosom of his Father and
his God.'

Much that is beside the mark has been written and
said about Pater's precise habits of composition. The
truth is that they were in no way unusual. The
common tradition is that he wrote words and sentences upon cards, and then when he had accumulated
a sufficient store, he dealt them out as though he were
playing a game of patience, and made them into a

species of mosaic. The real truth is much simpler. When he was studying a subject he took abundance of notes, but instead of making them in a note-book, he preferred slips of paper, for the greater convenience of sorting them, and arranged them in order so that they might illustrate the divisions of his subject.

Mr. Gosse, to whom was entrusted the task of deciphering the fragmentary manuscript of the "Pascal," gives one or two interesting instances of these notes, most of which are of the nature of passing thoughts, captured for future reference. One runs :—

"Something about the gloomy Byzantine archit., belfries, solemn night come in about the birds attracted by the Towers."

And again :—

"? did he suppose predestination to have taken place, only *after* the Fall ?"

When he had arranged his notes he began to write on ruled paper, leaving the alternate lines blank ; and in these spaces he would insert new clauses and descriptive epithets. Then the whole was re-copied, again on alternate lines, which would again be filled ; moreover, he often had an essay at this stage set up at his own expense in print, that he might better be able to judge of the effect; the same device that Tennyson so often used.

The work of writing grew easier to him as time went on. "Ah! it is much easier now," he said to Mr. Gosse, near the end of his life. "If I live long enough, no doubt I shall learn quite to like writing."

He was a regular rather than a hard worker. It was his habit for many years to devote two or three hours of the morning to writing, and he often wrote again for another hour in the afternoon. But he never

worked late at night; writing was to him an absorbing
and at the same time a fatiguing process, to be pursued
temperately and quietly. Some writers work for a time
as though possessed, fall into a profound exhaustion
when a book is finished, and then lie fallow for a time.
Such was never Pater's way. His writing was his
central concern; he loved it with an ever-growing love;
it formed the staple employment of his days; but his
friends say that there never was a man who seemed to
be always so free from preoccupation, so ready to put
his work aside, and enter into conversation of the most
trivial kind; there were no furtive glances at the clock,
none of the air of jealous if patient resignation, no
hunted sense of the desire to escape from interruption.

Again, too much emphasis has been laid upon the
conscious fatigue and exhaustion arising from his work.
He was not, like Flaubert, the racked and tortured
medium of his thought. He was a man of low physical
vitality, and he would sometimes half-humorously
lament the labour that his work cost him. But the toil
and the delight were inextricably intermingled; such
writing as Pater's with its subtle distinctions, its fine
metaphors, its delicate effects, its haunted richness, its
remote images, its liquid cadences, could never have
been produced except by one who tasted to the full
the artistic pleasure of elaborate workmanship. And
it is beyond all doubt that his work became to him in
increasing measure the mainspring of his life, a spring
of the purest joy.

One source of his concentrated strength was that he
never wasted time in experimental researches; he knew
his own mind; he knew exactly what interested him
and the limitations of his taste; thus he confined his
ideals to a restricted circle, and though perhaps losing
somewhat in catholicity of thought, he gained astonish-

ing depth and insight in certain specified directions. But he made no parade of omniscience. He used to say smilingly that it was such a relief to work hard at a subject and then forget all about it.

One of Pater's happiest accomplishments was his power of bringing up in a few words a figure or a scene, beautiful in itself and charged moreover with a further and remote significance, revealing as by a sudden glimpse or hint some solemn thought enshrined within the outer form. Thus he said once that churches where the Sacrament was reserved gave one the sense of a house where a dead friend lies; and again in a subtle allegory he touched the difference between Roman Catholicism with all its rich fabric of association and tradition, and Puritanism with its naked insistence on bare rectitude and rigid conduct. Roman Catholicism, he said, was like a table draped in fair linen, covered with lights and flowers and vessels of crystal and silver; while Puritanism was like the same table, after it had been cleared, serviceable enough, but without charm or grace. The essential form present in both; but the one furnished with rich and dainty accessories, the other unadorned and plain.

It may be said generally that richness under a severe restraint is the principal characteristic of Pater's style; but there are two or three special small characteristics, almost amounting to mannerisms, which may be noted in his writing. One is the natural result of his habit of composition; it is of overloading his sentences, of introducing long parentheses, of heaping fine detail together, which sometimes gives an impression of over-luxuriousness. Here is a typical sentence, out of one of the *Guardian Essays*, the review of Wordsworth :—

"An emanation, a particular spirit, belonged not to the moving leaves or water only, but to the distant peak arising suddenly, by some change of perspective, above the nearer horizon of the hills, to the passing space of light across the plain, to the lichened Druidic stone even, for a certain weird fellowship in it with the moods of men."

This sentence has every charm except the charm of perfect lucidity. But any one who enjoys the characteristic quality of Pater will be able to give its due value to the slight blurring of outline on which the charm to a certain extent depends.

Again, he was fond of beginning a sentence with the emphatic phrase, and thus inverting the clause. Where another writer would say, "That tale of hours, the long chanted English service, develops patience," Pater wrote: "It develops patience—that tale of hours, the long chanted English service." And again: "Horace!—he was, had been always, the idol of their school." And again: "Submissiveness!—It had the force of genius with Emerald Uthwart." Such sentences, occurring as a rule at the opening of a paragraph, are of constant occurrence. He had a fondness for points of exclamation: "How wretched! how fine! how inconceivably great and difficult!—not for him!" and his frequent introduction of the word "say!" with its stop breaking the continuity of the clause where an ordinary writer would use "for instance," is a favourite usage.

It is clear that he did not aim primarily at simplicity or lucidity. His style was deliberately adopted and practised, and he was careful to allow no influence whatever to interfere with it. He told Mr. Gosse that he had read scarcely a chapter of Stevenson, and not a line of Mr. Kipling.

"I feel, from what I hear about them," he said, "that they are strong; they might lead me out of my path. I want to go

on writing in my own way, good or bad. I should be afraid to
read Kipling, lest he should come between me and my page
next time I sat down to write."

His view was that slipshod impressionism, rough,
sketchy emphasis, was the literary fault of the time
which needed to be sternly resisted. Writing of a
serious kind, he felt, ought to be a strenuous, almost a
learned process. He wrote in one of the reviews he
contributed to the *Guardian* :—

"Well, the good quality of an age, the defect of which lies in
the direction of intellectual anarchy and confusion, may well
be eclecticism. . . . A busy age will hardly educate its
writers in correctness. Let its writers make time to write
English more as a learned language."

This thought had its effect upon his writing, even
when he was dealing with the apprehension of the
ordinary objects of sense and perception.

Great as was Pater's appreciation of nature, and fine
as was his perception of the quality and beauty of
landscape, it is almost always through a medium of
art that he beheld it. Nature is to him always a setting, a background, subordinated to the human interest.
The thought that men had laboured, painfully or
joyfully, over a building, or a picture, or a book, invested the result with a certain sacredness in his
eyes. The nearer that outward things approached
to humanity, the more they appealed to Pater. The
home, the house, the room, its furniture and decora-
tion, the garden, the pleasaunce, all these were nearer
to his heart than nature in her wilder and sterner aspects, because the thought and hand of humanity had
passed over them, writing its care and its dreams
legibly on cornice and lintel, on panel and beam, on
chest and press, on alley and bower, on border and

fountain.   When, as in "Duke Carl of Rosenmold," or
in "Sebastian van Storck," he describes the sunny
vine-clad country, or the lonely clump on the long hill
that seems to summon the vagrant foot thither, or the
frozen lake with the fur-clad skaters moving to and
fro, it is always with a sense of how such scenes might
have been painted. It is always nature seen through
the eye of the artist rather than in the mind of the
poet. There is little sense of expanse or largeness
about these natural touches ; they are rather caught at
salient points, in glimpses and vignettes, grouped and
isolated. It may be observed how rarely he alludes
to natural sounds ; these visions seem to be seen in a
reflective silence, recorded and represented by the
mind that has stored itself full of minute pictorial
impressions.   Pater went to nature, not in the
spirit of Wordsworth, to exult in the freedom, the
width, the tenderness, the energy, the vastness of it
all ; but rather as a great quarry of impressions,
through which he walked with a perceptive gaze,
selecting and detaching striking and charming effects,
which could afterwards be renewed and meditated
over in the home-keeping mind. None of his direct
nature-touches, beautiful as they are, are penetrated
with quite the same zest and emotion as his descriptions of nature when represented by some master-hand.
It was the penetration of nature by human personality
that gave it its value for Pater, its significance ; and
thus it comes about that his descriptions of scenes
always seem, so to speak, to have a frame about them.
He did not, like a poet, desire to escape from man to
nature ; but rather to suffuse nature at every point
with humanity, to judge of it, to feel its beauty, not
as the direct expression of the mind of God, but as it
affected and appealed to man.

It might have been imagined that so deliberate and
precise a craftsman, with so definite a theory of his
art, would perhaps have held on his way producing his
careful masterpieces, content to put it on record that
he had thought thus, and expressed it just so, content
that the beautiful thing should be formed and
fashioned, and made available for the use or delight
of any that followed the same or a like path among
the things of the soul. One could have supposed Pater
indifferent to criticism and censure, deeming it enough
not to be unfaithful to the heavenly vision. For to
him, doubtless, the first and chiefest pleasure lay in
the thrilling thought, that thought which sets the
writer's spirit all aglow, leaping into the mind, as it
does, with an almost physical shock, and opening up a
sudden vista of possibilities; as when a man, walking
in a wood, comes suddenly across a ride, and sees the
green space run to left and right, with its carpet of
flowers, its leafy walls. And next to that first and
sacred joy came the delight of the slow and careful
conception, tracing the development, restricting the
ramification, foreseeing the proportion. Then followed
the later joy, the gradual embroidery of the austere
outline, the laying of thread by thread, of colour by
colour; and then the final pleasure of strict revision,
of enriching the close texture, of strengthening the
languid cadence, of refining the refined epithet, the
eagerness to reach that impossible perfection that
seemed to recede even as he drew near.

Yet even to a craftsman thus wholeheartedly intent
upon his work, there is a satisfaction in publication
which is like the framing of a picture. The book with
its white margins, its delicate sprinkling of ornament,
its headings and mottoes, all this is the symbol of completion, of an end attained. There is a further delight

still in the possibility of becoming thus the companion
of the imagined reader; to be held in unknown hands
and scanned by gentle eyes; to appeal to kindred
natures, kindly and generous persons; the thought of
this to one like Pater, who had found so many in the
world whom he could love, and to whom human relations had always so deep and sacred a significance,
was full of a potent attraction.   But one is perhaps
surprised to learn that he was also deeply sensitive to
adverse criticism; that he felt about the harsh and summary treatment of his books, especially when they were
misrepresented or misunderstood, something of what
the old Psalmist felt, when he prayed that his darling
might be delivered from the power of the dog.   There
were times when he suffered acutely from the attacks
of critics, as when the exquisite and elaborate Essay on
"Style" was treated as incomprehensible and affected;
when he declared with desolate conviction that his
pleasure in writing was gone, and that he could never
resume his work.   Only those nearest to him knew of
these dark moods of discouragement, because he was
not one who took the world into his confidence;
indeed, to those who were without, his gentle and
equable manner seemed to bear witness to a tranquillity of mind, which indeed he sedulously practised,
although he never attained the deep serenity of which
he was in search.

It is a curious fact that Pater showed no precocious
signs, in boyhood and youth, of a desire to write.
Those in whose blood stirs the creative impulse, the
literary energy, feel the thrill as a rule very early,
and cover paper diligently from their first years.   But
Pater's family cannot remember that he ever showed
any particular tendency to write.   He never wrote
poetry in childhood, except a few humorous verses,

long lost and forgotten; later on he made some verse-translations from Goethe, Alfred de Musset, and the Greek Anthology; and this abstention from the composition of verse is a remarkable fact in the case of one whose prose is so essentially poetical. It is common to differentiate the prose of poets, as in the case of Dryden, Keats, Shelley, Matthew Arnold, and others, from the prose of those who have never attempted to write in verse; it is thought that it has a greater precision, a sonorous richness, a more vivid colouring. If Pater had ever practised the art of poetry, it would be easy to point to his prose as a supreme instance of these qualities, because, quite apart from its luxurious prodigality, both of epithet and image, it has a strong, rhythmical, almost metrical movement in places. But, as a matter of fact, his chief characteristics, as a prose-writer, came to him late. As a rule, the makers of gorgeous and exquisite prose have begun by erring on the side of diffuseness and ornament, and have chastened their style into due proportion and lucidity. But Pater's earliest writings, which seem to have been essays for Societies, have none of the later charm; they tend to be austere, hard, and even dry. Neither did he arrive at his plentiful and magnificent vocabulary, as some writers have done, by the production of large masses of writing that never see the light, in which their hand has learned firmness of outline, and their teeming brain the power of summoning the supremely appropriate word from a suspended cloud of more or less suitable language. His method was far otherwise. At one time he applied himself daily for some months to translating a page of Sainte-Beuve or Flaubert, and this seems to have been his only exercise. His prose steadily grew in volume and depth; and the one serious fault of his writing, the tendency that his sentences have to become long and involved, did not diminish. What he did gain as years went on was a refined and surprising power over words, a power of condensing an elaborate effect into a single haunting sentence which suggests rather than reveals. His work was always the result of much patient and unseen labour; but though he revised carefully and jealously enough in many cases, his richness was not derived in reality so much from these stippled effects, as from the fulness of mind out of which he wrote. Any one who has ever gone over the same ground as Pater, and studied the same authorities, will be amazed to find how con- scientiously and diligently the material has all been employed; not by elaborately amplifying detail, but by condensing an abundance of scattered points into a single illuminating hint, a poignant image, an apt illustration. He was entirely remote from those easy superficial writers who generalise from insufficient pre- mises, and bridge the gaps in their knowledge by grace- ful fabrics of words. All Pater's work was strongly focussed; he drew the wandering and scattered rays, as through a crystal lens, into a burning and convergent point of light. Not to travel far for in- stances, the essay on Leonardo is a perfect example of this. The writing is so delicate, so apparently fanciful, that it is only through a careful study of the available tradition that one comes to realise how minute is the knowledge that furnishes out these gemmed and luminous sentences. It is true that his knowledge is not pedantically applied, that he concerns himself little with minute and technical questions of art-criticism; but I conceive that Pater's attempt was always to discern the inner beauty, the essence of the thing; to disentangle the personality, the humanity of the artist, rather than to classify or analyse the work. And so it comes about that his art-criticism is essentially a creative thing, that adds little to the historical aspect of the development of art, and falls indeed at times into positive error; the training, the severe observation, the cultivated instinct is there, but it is relegated, so to speak, to an ante-room, while the spirit is led to apprehend something of the mysterious issues of art, initiated into the secret appreciation of beauty, and drawn to worship in the darkened innermost shrine. There is always something holy, even priestly, about Pater's attitude to art. It insists upon the initial critical training, the necessity of ordered knowledge; but it leaves this far behind; it passes beyond the nice apprehension of eye, the cultivated sense of line and colour, the exact discrimination of style and medium, into a remote and poetical region. Such secrets cannot be explained or even analysed; they cannot be communicated to those that are without; they must be emotionally and mystically apprehended, by the soul rather than by the mind.

It was this secret vision, this inner enlightening, on which Pater had set his heart, and which he sought for urgently and diligently. He loved the symbol, not for itself alone, but for the majesty which it contained, the hidden light which it guarded. It is in this region alone that he seems to wear an absorbed and pontifical air, not with the false sacerdotal desire to enhance personal impressiveness and private dignity, through the ministry of divine powers and holy secrets, but with the unconscious emotion of one whose eyes behold great wonders enacting themselves upon the bodiless air, which the dull and the contemptuous may not discern.

It remains to attempt to indicate Pater's position in later English literature, and his philosophy, or rather his

point of view, by summarising what has already, it is to
be hoped, been made clear by analysis.

In literature he practically struck out a new line.
The tendency of the best prose-writers of the century
had been, as a rule, to employ prose in a prosaic manner.
Landor had aimed at a Greek austerity of style.
Macaulay had brought to perfection a bright hard-
balanced method of statement, like the blowing of sharp
trumpets. This was indeed the prose that had recommended itself to the taste of the early Victorians ; it
was full of a certain sound and splendour ; it rolled
along in a kind of impassioned magnificence ; but the
object of it was to emphasise superficial points in an
oratorical manner, to produce a glittering panorama
rich in detail; it made no appeal to the heart or the
spirit, awaking at best a kind of patriotic optimism, a
serene self-glorification.

Carlyle had written from the precisely opposite point
of view ; he was overburdened with passionate metaphysics which he involved in a texture of rugged
Euphuism, intensely mannerised. But he had no
catholicity of grasp, and his picturesqueness had little
subtlety or delicacy, because his intense admiration for
certain qualities and types blinded him to finer shades
of character. There was no restraint about his style,
and thus his enthusiasm turned to rant, his statement
of preferences degenerated into a species of frantic
bombast.

With these Pater had nothing in common; the
writers with whom he is more nearly connected are
Charles Lamb, De Quincey, Newman, and Ruskin. He
was akin to Charles Lamb in the delicacy of touch, the
subtle flavour of language ; and still more in virtue of
his tender observation, his love of interior domestic
life. He has a certain nearness to De Quincey in the

impassioned autobiographical tendency, the fondness
for retrospect, which Pater considered the characteristic of the poetical temperament. He is akin to Newman in respect of the restraint, the economy of effect,
the perfect suavity of his work; but none of these probably exerted any very direct influence upon him.
Ruskin perhaps alone of the later prose-writers had a
permanent effect on the style of Pater. He learnt from
Ruskin to realise intensely the suggestiveness of art,
to pursue the subjective effect upon the mind of the
recipient; but though the rich and glowing style of
Ruskin enlarged the vocabulary of Pater, yet we can
trace the time when he parted company with him, and
turned aside in the direction of repression rather than
volubility, of severity rather than prodigality.

It may be said, then, that Pater really struck out a
new line in English prose, working on the principles
enunciated by Flaubert in a widely different region.
The essence of his attempt was to produce prose that
had never before been contemplated in English, full
of colour and melody, serious, exquisite, ornate. He
devoted equal pains both to construction and orna-
mentation. Whether he is simple and stately, whether
he is involved and intricate, he has the contrast always
in view. His object was that every sentence should
be weighted, charged with music, haunted with echoes;
that it should charm and suggest, rather than convince
or state. The danger of the perfection to which he
attained is the danger of over-influence, seductive
sweetness; the value is to suggest the unexplored
possibilities of English as a vehicle for a kind of prose
that is wholly and essentially poetical. The triumph
of his art is to be metrical without metre, rhythmical
without monotony. There will, of course, always be
those whom this honeyed, laboured cadence will affect

painfully with a sense of something stifling and over-perfumed; and, indeed, the merits of a work of art can never be established by explanation or defended by argument; but to such as can apprehend, feel, enjoy, there is the pleasure of perfected art, of language that obeys and enriches the thought, of calculated effect, of realisation, with a supreme felicity of the intention of the writer.

One does not praise his works as the perfection of style; there is a limpidity and lucidity of prose style—prose as used by Newman, by Matthew Arnold, by Ruskin in chastened moods,—to which no style that depends upon elaborateness and artifice can attain; but it may fairly be claimed for Pater that he realised his own conception of perfection. The style is heavy with ornament, supple with artifice. It is not so much a picture as an illumination. For sunlight there is stiff burnished gold; it is full of gorgeous conceits, jewelled phrases; it has no ease or simplicity; it is all calculated, wrought up, stippled; but it must be considered from that point of view; it must be appraised rather than criticised, accepted rather than judged.

To feel the charm it is necessary to be, to some extent, in sympathy with the philosophy of Pater. We see in him a naturally sceptical spirit, desiring to plunge beneath established systems and complacent explanations; and this, in common with an intense sensibility to every hint and intimation of beauty, apprehended in a serious and sober spirit; not the spirit that desires to possess itself of the external elements, but to penetrate the essential charm. Yet it is not the patient and untroubled beauty of nature, of simple effects of sun and shade, of great mountains, of wide plains, but of a remote and symbolical beauty, seen by glimpses and in corners, of which he was in search—beauty with which is mixed a certain strangeness and mystery, that suggests an inner and a deeper principle behind, intermingled with a sadness, a melancholy that is itself akin to beauty.

There is always an interfusion of casuistical and metaphysical thought with Pater's apprehension of beauty; he seems to be ever desirous to draw near to the frankness, the unashamed happiness of the Greek spirit, but to be for ever held back by a certain fence of scepticism, a malady of thought.

Yet the beauty of which he takes account is essentially of a religious kind; it draws the mind to the further issue, the inner spirit. All the charm of ritual and ceremonial in worship has for Pater an indefinable and constant attraction. He is for ever recurring to it, because it seems to him to interpret and express an emotion, a need of the human spirit, whose concern is to comprehend if it can what is the shadowy figure, the mysterious will, that moves behind the world of sight and sense.

We can trace the progress of thought in the case of Pater as clearly as it is possible to trace the thought of any recent writer; though reticent and even suavely ironical in talk, he was in his writings at once self-centred and *intime*. His own emotions, his own pre-occupations were absorbingly important to him; yet while he shrank from giving them facile utterance, he was irresistibly impelled to take the world into his confidence. He had none of the frank egotism of Wordsworth, none of the complacent belief in the interest of his revelations of himself; and yet there is no writer that speaks more persistently and self-consciously of his own point of view. He made little attempt to pass outside of it, and hardly disguised what he would fain have concealed. The instinct,

indeed, for expression triumphs at every point over
the instinct for reticence.

We see the silent, self-contained boyhood, the
intellectual awakening, the absorption in metaphysics,
and their abandonment, the eager pursuit of recondite
beauty, that from the days of his maturity never left
him; we see in the candour, the urbanity, the delicate
and gentle outlook, the intellectual strenuousness of
his heroes, a reflection of his own personal ideal. We
see how he was led to trust personal intuitions rather
than intellectual processes; to listen rather for the
simpler, sweeter message which comes from life, from
experience, from sympathy, than to obey the logical
conclusions of reason, which indeed arrives so soon at
the consciousness of its own limitations; we see that
he determined that the function of reason was rather
to keep judgment suspended; that it should be applied
as a solvent alike to philosophical and religious
systems; but that the spirit should not thus be
bound; that reason should indeed erect the framework
of the house, its walls and doorways—and that then its
work was done; while the spirit should dwell within,
drawing its strength from the tender observation of
humanity, from humble service, from quiet companionship, while it should all the time keep its eyes open to
any faintest message flashed from afar, whether it
came through glance or word, through book or
picture, through charm of form or colour, from tower
or tree, from the clear freshness of the solitary dawn,
or from the orange sunset dying softly over wide,
glimmering fields.

" Behold, this dreamer cometh!" So, with an
envious contempt, the petty-minded scheming brethren
of the inspired child beloved of God greeted him, as he

came in unsuspecting innocence to join them in the
field. He was to learn, even in the tender days of
boyhood, how heavy a burden that secret knowledge
was to be, that inheritance of the inner and deeper
sight which could pierce behind the veil of mortality.
If he could have foreseen the weary way he was to
travel to the calm and prosperous eminence of later
years, would he not have hidden the visions which he
revealed so guilelessly ?   Not even the certainty of
the honour and comfort of the future would have
made amends for the loneliness, the malignity of the
labyrinth which he was so gently and faithfully to
thread. This power of inner sight, this perception of
the essence of things, must always, it seems, bring its
possessor a certain sadness, a certain isolation. The
prosperous worldly spirits, that swim so vigorously on
the surface of things, have always a suspicion, a jealousy,
a contempt for one who dives deeper, and brings back
tidings of the strange secrets that the depth holds.
But if such clear-sighted spirits go tranquilly upon their
way, and utter fearlessly the truth they discern, though
the way be difficult and arduous, the honour comes at
last, unsought, unprized. And it is well perhaps that
the conquest is so hard, because if the victory came at
once, with it would doubtless come the relish for the
easy, the obvious triumph ; but by the time that it
arrives, the pure spirit, chastened and refined, has
reached a region where the only pleasure that fame
brings is the knowledge that the truth has somewhat
prevailed. There is no taint of personal complacency,
no luxurious yielding to lower satisfactions, nothing
but the unstained delight that the mystery, discerned
and interpreted, is bearing in other hearts its rich and
reviving fruits.

Such is the life that I have attempted to depict. It

is the life of one who, through a dreamful and un-praised boyhood, through a silent and undistinguished youth, gradually discerned a principle in things; learned to see, with an impassioned zest, the truth that, in art and life alike, the victory is with those who attain to a certain patient and appreciative attitude of soul; who learn through careful toil, through much sorting of accumulated thought and expression, to dis-criminate between what is facile, impressive, specious, and what is deep, permanent, sincere. No taste can of course be wholly catholic; it is swayed by instinct, prepossession, and preference. But the point is, in however limited a sphere, to be able to detect with unfailing certainty the true quality of things.

He of whom we speak achieved this art of subtle discrimination, a gift which is shared by dumb and learned connoisseurs; but above this rise a few, who can not only by a trained instinct recognise what is perfect, but who can express their methods and powers so that canons and standards can be formed. Then to but one or two in a generation is given a further gift: the creative, the poetical power to express in language of high and haunting beauty the deepest mysteries of art; who can not only praise in noble and inspiring terms the beautiful thing, the exquisite work, the flashing thought, but can disen-tangle the very essence of the secret, establish remote and subtle connections, and open, if only for one glorious instant, a door into the inner shrine, showing a vision of awful angels, bent on high service, interpret-ing the loud crying of mysterious voices, echoing the rising strain that fills the golden-roofed palace, and giving perhaps an awe-struck glimpse of the presence that sits enthroned there.

But not always on these august heights does the

haunted spirit dwell. There is a spell unknown to those who live the eager life of affairs, who dwell in crowded cities, or who carry the busy, scheming mind abroad with them into lonelier places; the spell that broods over the wooded valley with its hazel-hidden stream, where the bird sings among the thickets; the spell that lies behind the dark tree-trunks of the grove that bar the smouldering sunset with shafts of shade; that trembles in the green twilight when the stars begin to glimmer, and the winds are hushed. This too, and its appeal to the heart of man, the tinge that it lends to his dreams, the passionate desire to record, to represent, to give permanence of form to the hurrying moment—all this needs to be interpreted as well.

But here, to the true prophet of these mysteries, the thought that must be caught and touched and given shape, is not so much the mystery itself—for that is dark and not to be apprehended—but the thrill which such visions have communicated to the hearts of other pilgrims, who have fared eagerly and sadly through the world before us, and have passed into the darkness, just leaving, in written signs and pictured symbols, the traces of the passion, the desire, the yearning that such things have brought them. Such a task as this—this piecing together of personality, this testing of recorded impressions, this imbuing of ancient, half-faded dreams with the sanguine vitality, the eager hope of to-day, needs one who is not less a poet than a critic. The dreamer that comes thus must not be absorbed in his own fruitful visions, but must be able, by an energy of sympathy, a lucid purity of soul, to enter no less eagerly into the dim and far-reaching visions of other inspired spirits.

INDEX

221

199 ; habits of composition, 201-6 ; significant writing, 204 ; principal characteristics of style, 204, 215 ; typical sentence, 204-5 ; did not read Stevenson or Kipling, 205-6 ; always regards nature as a background, 206-7 ; sensitiveness to adverse criticism, 209 ; no precocious desire to write, 209-10 ; abstains from verse composition, 210 ; late development of style, 210-1 ; attitude towards art, 212 ; position in later English literature, 212-15 ; writing contrasted with Carlyle's, 213 ; as a writer akin to Charles Lamb, 213 ; a dreamer, 217-20.

Pater's friends, 20, 21.

Pater, William Thompson (brother), 2.

Pattison, Mark (Rector of Lincoln), 21, 37, 190, 192.

Pensées (Pascal), 173.

"Philosophers, The Three" ("The Chaldean Sages"), (picture), 50.

Plato, 165, 167.

Plato and Platonism, 20, 54, 58, Jowett's admiration of, 58 ; began to appear (1892), 156 ; 159 ; eventually published (1893), 162 ; 163-8.

Poe, Edgar Allan, criticism of, 23.

Purgatory (C. L. Shadwell's trans. of), 159.

Q

Queen's College (Oxford), description of, 8.

R

Renaissance, Studies in the History of the (with "Preface" and

"Conclusion '), 1st ed. (1873), 2nd and 3rd (1877), 32-3 ; 35, 36—

"Conclusion," 45, reason for exclusion from 2nd ed. of *Studies*, etc., 46, 47-8 ; principle of selection explained, 37 ; Lady Dilke's criticism of, 37-8 ; 49-51, 52, 59, 162.

"Aucassin and Nicolette" ("Two Early French Stories") (1873), 32-3, 38.

"Joachim du Bellay," 33, 44-5.

"*Leonardo da Vinci, Notes on*" (1869), 32, 41, 42-3, 49, 177.

"Luca della Robbia," 33, 39.

"Michelangelo, Poetry of," 32, 39-40.

"Pico della Mirandola" (1871), 32, 38-9.

"Sandro Botticelli, A fragment on," 32, 39.

"School of Giorgione, The" (1877), 43-4, 50-1, 66.

"Winckelmann" (1866), 27-31, 45.

Robert Elsmere (Mrs. H. Ward), 57, review on, 119, 198-9.

"Rossetti, Dante Gabriel" (Ward's *English Poets*), essay on, 86-7.

Ruskin, John, 7, 51, 163, 185, 214-15.

S

"Shadows of Events" (*Gaston de Latour*), 140.

Shadwell, 2.

Shadwell, Dr. Charles Lancelot (Pater's lifelong friend), 9, 10 *n.* ; as literary executor, 21.

"Solomon, The Judgment of" (picture), 51.

Stevenson, R. L., 205-6.

"Stormy Landscape, The" ("Ad-

Printed by T. and A. Constable, Printers to His Majesty
at the Edinburgh University Press

𝔈𝔫𝔤𝔩𝔦𝔰𝔥 𝔐𝔢𝔫 𝔬𝔣 𝔏𝔢𝔱𝔱𝔢𝔯𝔰

NEW SERIES

Crown 8vo. Gilt tops. Flat backs. 2s. net each.

GEORGE ELIOT. By Sir LESLIE STEPHEN, K.C.B.

HAZLITT. By AUGUSTINE BIRRELL, K.C.

MATTHEW ARNOLD. By HERBERT W. PAUL.

RUSKIN. By FREDERIC HARRISON.

TENNYSON. By Sir ALFRED LYALL.

RICHARDSON. By AUSTIN DOBSON.

BROWNING. By G. K. CHESTERTON.

CRABBE. By ALFRED AINGER.

FANNY BURNEY. By AUSTIN DOBSON.

JEREMY TAYLOR. By EDMUND GOSSE.

ROSSETTI. By A. C. BENSON.

MARIA EDGEWORTH. By the Hon. EMILY LAWLESS.

HOBBES. By Sir LESLIE STEPHEN, K.C.B.

ADAM SMITH. By FRANCIS W. HIRST.

THOMAS MOORE. By STEPHEN GWYNN.

SYDNEY SMITH. By GEORGE W. E. RUSSELL.

EDWARD FITZGERALD. By A. C. BENSON.

ANDREW MARVELL. By AUGUSTINE BIRRELL, K.C.

SIR THOMAS BROWNE. By EDMUND GOSSE.

WALTER PATER. By A. C. BENSON.

MRS. GASKELL. By CLEMENT SHORTER.

CHARLES KINGSLEY. By G. K. CHESTERTON.

SHAKESPEARE. By WALTER RALEIGH.

JAMES THOMSON. By G. C. MACAULAY.

MACMILLAN AND CO., LTD., LONDON